Oxstalls Library
University of Gloucestershire
Oxstalls Campus, Oxstalls Lane
Longlevens, Gloucester
Gloucestershire
GL2 9HW

Praise for Professor Colin Turner's work

'I sincerely hope millions read Colin Turner's inspirational books'
Sir Michael Grylls MP

'Success in business is about releasing potential – Colin's definitive book does that' *Ken Moran, Chairman, Pfizer UK*

'Highly researched yet intuitive' *Neil Holloway, MD, Microsoft UK*

'Where others promise, Colin delivers' *Adrian Hosford, Director, BT*

'East meets West for successful business'
His Excellency, Ma Zengang, Chinese Ambassador

'Powerfully provokes your thinking'
Jeff Papows, president and CEO Lotus Corporation

'Practical ideas; simple yet so effective'
Margaret Chapman, MD, Investors in People

'Colin's philosophy works'
Chris Cowdray, CEO, Claridges

'Compulsory reading'
Dr Marilyn Orcharton, Founder of Denplan

'Straight to the point' *Benny Higgins, Director, The Royal Bank of Scotland*

'Your work is a powerful conduit for success'
Sir Douglas Morpeth, Chairman Clerical Medical

'A commonsense and principled approach that brings lasting results'
George McWatters, Founder, HTV

'Colin brings the key fundamentals of success in an inspiring yet practical way' *Nigel Swabey, Founder, The Innovations Group; CEO Scots & Stowe*

'The philosophy for the 21st Century'
Vera Peiffer, Author of 'Positive Thinking'

'A first class informative keynote, Colin really does his research. All our members talked about his thought-provoking practical concepts for weeks afterwards.' *Michael Fleisher, President, Gartner*

'To hold us enthralled for I hour is one thing; but for 2 is outstanding. Colin's interactive, inspirational and absorbing presentation for our Forum was outstanding.' *David Pulman, President GMS, GlaxoSmithKline*

'Let me congratulate YOU on the magnificent presentation. I have had tons of positive feed-back. You have certainly carved your name into the core management of ASSA ABLOY' *Bo Dankis, CEO Assa Abloy*

'Thank you for an outstanding keynote – it was the highlight of our partners' conference.' *Vujovic Branislav, Sales Director EMC*

'The most thought-provoking 30 minutes of the two-day conference.' *Andrew Higgins, Brand & Communications Director, Shell Global Solutions*

Colin Turner's work hooks like a thriller you can't put down...that it is also engrossing inspiring and upbeat makes it essential reading for everyone with a job. *Time Out*

'I was delighted with Colin Turner's latest book' *Sir John Harvey-Jones*

'Creates positive results for business' *Evening Standard*

'Highly recommended' *Financial Times*

'Sound Advice' *Daily Mail*

'Colin's been there and knows what he is talking about' *Success Today*

'Crammed full of seriously good advice'*The Irish News*

What Turner preaches he has practised out there *Sunday Independent*

The thinking person's Little Book of Calm *Belfast Telegraph*

'Truly inspiring...I doubt very much whether anyone's life will remain unchanged' *Here's Health*

'What Colin has to share is worth reading *Business Age*

'Dramatic, though-provoking, influential' *BBC*

COLIN TURNER

Passion v Pension

DEVELOPING CORPORATE ENTREPRENEURSHIP

'Europe's foremost teacher of business success'
Business Age

**21st
Century
Books**

Passion v Pension

Developing Corporate Entrepreneurship

Copyright © Colin Turner 2004

The right of Colin Turner to be identified as the Author of the Work has been asserted
by him in accordance with the Copyright, Design and Patents Act 1988

First Published in Great Britain in 2004 by
21st Century Books UK Ltd
30 Queen Square, Bristol, BS1 4ND

www.21stcenturybooks.uk.co.
service@21stcenturybooks.uk.com

Cover Design by Dick Evry, Bath
Printed and bound in the UK by The Bath Press,
Lower Bristol Road, Bath, England

British Library Cataloguing in Publication
Data available

ISBN: 1-904956-03-3

Colin Turner is the author of 15 bestsellers published in 30 languages, including the Japan no 1: Born to Succeed; and the executive coaching series: The Teachings of Billionaire Yen Tzu. Described by Time as 'a leading authority on business, lifestyle & management'; he advises FTSE 100 and Fortune 500 Companies and is a thought-provoking keynote speaker at conferences. He can be contacted through: service@21stcenturybooks.uk.com

His books include:

BORN TO SUCCEED

THE EUREKA PRINCIPLE

FINANCIAL FREEDOM

MADE FOR LIFE

SWIMMING WITH PIRANHA MAKES YOU HUNGRY

THE BUSINESS PILGRIM'S PROGRESS

LEAD TO SUCCEED

THE TEACHINGS OF BILLIONAIRE YEN TZU VOLUME I

THE TEACHINGS OF BILLIONAIRE YEN TZU VOLUME II

THE 21ST CENTURY THOUGHTOLOGY BRIEFCASE SERIES VOLUMES I-VI

Contents

Passion v Pension

DEVELOPING CORPORATE ENTREPRENEURSHIP

Author's Note

THE PURPOSE OF THIS BOOK is to show how to develop within established organisations those entrepreneurial attributes that were originally instrumental in founding the business but which have, in the majority of them, been allowed to atrophy. It is not intended for budding entrepreneurs who are seeking to establish their own business. And indeed there is a clear distinction between the start-up entrepreneur and the entrepreneurially-minded leader.

The former involves one or more individuals that seek out opportunity in the free-enterprise market. The latter is not so concerned about finding opportunities, than creating an organisation that stimulates entrepreneurial thinking and specific follow-through action as a matter of course. The former will seldom risk their own capital on their ventures and indeed the majority of new start-up businesses continue to close with losses to venture capitalists and other various stakeholders. Those that do succeed, however, seem to do so because they engage certain entrepreneurial characteristics while at the same time following proven business principles that actually stimulate innovation. These characteristics, that are clearly essential for future organisational leaders, are detailed within this book.

It is now accepted that the most important competitive and growth factor that a corporation possesses is the development of its people. Yet, few organisations have been fully able to embrace what is required. Consequently, they are still struggling to meet the challenges that local and global markets increasingly demand. This is despite their various well-meaning development initiatives to improve innovation, communication and effectiveness and, above all, to instil a sense of ownership and customer service ethos.

It is also accepted that entrepreneurs today have a far greater certainty that the development of their ideas will be both profitable and sustainable when they acquire management skills, than those entrepreneurs who do not acquire such skills. It is not accepted, however, that senior executives with major organisational responsibilities must in turn acquire entrepreneurial attributes. Such a balance of attributes is essential today for capitalising on previously overlooked, as well as new, opportunities; to winning more business and increasing market share. Most organisations, however, severely lack this balance, to their detriment.

Creating entrepreneurial leadership within a structured and seemingly stable environment, such as an established organisation, may sound like a contradiction in terms. But it is upon such paradoxes that future organisations will rely, for the degree to which entrepreneurial leadership exists within organisations will be in direct proportion to the organisation's growth.

Though many organisations may enjoy success today, they will quite simply not survive in the increasingly competitive global market of tomorrow. Size and brand may allow the opportunity to be capitalized on but such opportunity arrives usually on a plate and involves only a small amount of people potential and organizational resources. Unless an organisation seeks to release all of its potential and utilise effectively its resources, it will not be successfully fulfilling its purpose even though it has the capabilities to do so.

Throughout my career, the research I have undertaken has persistently interacted with my practical business experience to uncover what causes some individuals to lack the confidence to succeed while others are confident of success, despite enduring failure; what motivates individuals to become employees, employers, managers, entrepreneurs and leaders; and what makes certain people achieve and innovate more than other colleagues, relatives or partners.

My observations and study have revealed certain insights. The very foundation of personal success is through continuous self-development, though seldom are we aware of the essential tools required for such an important challenge. Similarly, the very foundation of business success is through understanding, developing and practicing entrepreneurial characteristics. Indeed every small business and large organisation owes its original existence to entrepreneurship. Furthermore entrepreneurship offers by far the best way to develop individuals. Confident, self-assured individuals able to align what they do with who they are ensure both personal and business success.

Having had the opportunity to study, write, research, advise, consult and learn with some of the world's leading organisations, and to have also experienced building a few multi-million dollar entrepreneurial enterprises from start-up, there are three further points to share. First, my personal passion continues to be one of inspiring others to fulfil their potential. I believe wholehearted in the principle that the best way to serve yourself, to strive to be the best you can be, is through serving others. Our formative years, where we have the opportunity to learn to serve others, be creative, lead others, and finish what we start, are sadly lost in learning how to get by, rather than how to get on.

Perhaps the most critically important time of our developmental growth is exactly that – critical. All too often we become experts in spotting what is wrong with an argument rather than what is right. And because we habitually strive to behave in a manner that is consistent with what we are most comfortable with, we apply the same critical eye with regard to new ideas, new innovations and creativity. Any form of 'entrepreneurial thinking' or 'innovative leadership' is, in our conditioned opinion, probably best avoided.

This lack of entrepreneurial thinking leads to the second point. For 30 years I have increasingly observed that the organisational world is basically comprised of a series of meetings, far too many of which achieve absolutely nothing. Many large organisations today, incredible as it may sound, seem to be successful in spite of themselves. But when we define success in terms of how much they fully utilise their assets and fulfil their potential, then many, by definition, are not succeeding.

Even more amazing is that, in sharing this with executive boards, senior management conferences, and academic institutions, few have ever challenged it. Indeed, on the contrary, most have agreed. From small, but essential (yet not followed through and therefore lost forever), actions discussed in a team meeting to major strategic messages delivered at expensive conferences (but not passed on and therefore remaining un-communicated), too many highly trained and experienced movers of business think and therefore act simply as hired hand. Such people only do what they believe their brief, remit, role or job responsibility expects of them – by their own perception of course. One of the major precepts of this book is to learn how to think entrepreneurially instead of employee-rially.

The third point is that I have been astounded over the years at the responses I have received to the simple question posed to bright graduates and highly experienced managers alike: 'Why does an organisation employ you?' Varying from: 'Because I have a good CV / MBA / degree / experience / education / background etc.,' to: 'I can manage people effectively / administrate / control systems etc.,' most responses refer to normal requirements. An organisation does not, should not at any rate, employ highly qualified or experienced personnel because of qualifications or experience. That is what may attract them to you, but heaven help both them and you if that is their sole motivation. The only reason that should count is because of the added value you are able to bring to an organisation.

A business operates successfully when it makes measurable and incremental returns for its products or services. Corporate success demands seven skills from an 'in'-coming executive:

1. Insight for what the future will be;
2. Intuition for making right decisions;
3. Initiative for acting effectively;
4. Innovation for creating differently;
5. Integrity for following through correctly;
6. Individuality for accepting ownership; and
7. Interdependence for applying the above as a colleague within a team.

An organisation should choose personnel so that it can be more successful, to work with them in common focus towards a shared vision. Those corporations that choose to perceive personnel as operators to established processes; and those 'employees' who continue to perceive what they do as a reward for their qualification or experience, will in both cases continue to get by, rather than on, until the need for survival forces them to change.

Change is constant, coined Disraeli, yet few established organisations embrace the full meaning of the expression, even though change budgets are often larger than the revenue of some small countries. Professional complacency, lack of innovation and avoidance of ownership can no longer be allowed to be as rife as it is in business today. Those organisations seeking to generate positive growth for all their involved stakeholders will have to develop a real equilibrium between entrepreneurial thinking and their established structure. In the global-local-global business arena few business models are today relevant.

Perhaps the most appropriate model is the working gyroscope because of its ability to stay in balance irrespective of its angle or direction. Such a model, for example, positively ensures that our own planet maintains perfect universal balance. Conversely a gyroscope's negative feedback keeps a projectile in balance and focused on target. Such a constant, yet ever-moving, model is the perfect metaphor for creating the entrepreneurial culture within the established organisation. With each strategic direction the whole company moves while still maintaining balance.

Passion v Pension is the third in a trilogy. When Born to Succeed, the first in the trilogy, went on to be published in some 25 languages including reaching no 1 in Japan, it became clear that the message the book carried inspired many individuals to set up their own businesses and many organisations to develop their people. Adhering to the Principle that we cannot complain about the street until first our own house is in order, the book clearly laid a path for releasing potential in the individual.

The second of the trilogy, The Eureka Principle, shared how to actually align what we personally are, with what we professionally do. Through the blending of eastern philosophy with contemporary western experience into a practical format it sought to provide those ingredients vital for organisational change. Again the demand was clear. I received many enquiries from diverse corporations as to how the philosophy and ideas I expounded could be further developed, in established and hierarchal structures, to create an entrepreneurial organisation. It was this evolving demand that motivated me to research and write Passion v Pension. The fact is that in each of our hearts we have a passion to chase. Yet, we become far too concerned about securing our pension. There is infinitely more security, however, in chasing our passion than worrying about our pension. And when we express ourselves within the business arena both individual and corporate potential are released.

In the east there is wise aphorism that the best master never loses his passion for learning. For the moment he stops being a student he brings his evolution to a standstill and can no longer lead others. In the west there is an increasing understanding that the best organisations must be places of learning or they will not progress. Both these factors are vital for success because the best way to learn is to teach. Leaders must therefore be students and teachers making certain that their organisations are environments conducive to developing people-potential to the full.

Without doubt the successful organisation tomorrow will develop entrepreneurial leadership today and the following chapters sequentially show how to create such corporate entrepreneurship. For the future is not what it used to be; it belongs to those organisations that are friendly yet fearless, experienced yet innovative and established yet entrepreneurial.

Colin Turner

Part One:
Warriors v Worriers

Chapter 1
Recreating the spirit of Entrepreneurship

Chapter 2
Evolving Employeeship to Entrepreneurship

Chapter 1
Recreating the spirit of Entrepreneurship

WHY ARE WE IN BUSINESS? What are the reasons organisations are founded? Which motivations cause some to become great while others less so? How is it that some are successful despite poor planning, when others with good strategy are mediocre?

Born to Succeed opened with Plato's remark: *'that which is created must of necessity be created for a cause'* indicating the underlying precept of the book that *'our purpose is to realise our potential.'* Irrespective of whether we are aware of it, all of us share a primary yearning to know that we count for something. Each of us has a need to feel part of a worthwhile cause, to have a sense of purpose that gives our life and what we *do* meaning. When life lacks meaning, or direction, our frustrations drive us more than our aspirations are able to motivate us. We may recognise the importance of knowing what our core values and beliefs are. But do we really live by them? Are we too busy making the right moves to be guided by what motivates us?

What are organisations? They start out as legal documents. What makes them live and breathe are the people who first create them. Such people are not necessarily born leaders;

have had a great idea; want to empire build; or make a fortune. They are ordinary people that are motivated by a purpose. What makes an organisation grow is when it adheres to the original philosophy that lies behind its fundamental reason for existence. It follows that *the purpose of an organisation is to realise its potential.* And the realising of its potential lies in the strength of its purpose. Though strategies may adapt accordingly with evolving market conditions, when purpose and core values prevail the organisation remains a great place to work and something people are proud to be a part of.

This may sound ideological, yet it is exactly how the lasting and really successful organisations of the past developed. If we take the view that the best motive for growing organisations is for what they stand for, it changes our perspective on why we are in business and why we have organisations. And it is the purpose of this book to show how to create the entrepreneurial climate and warrior characteristics that were, and still are, essential to an organisation's successful growth.

Why Entrepreneurial Organisations?

I have chosen the titles of warriors and worriers to make the distinction between the entrepreneurial-minded and the non-entrepreneurial-minded organisation. Because it is ultimately people's beliefs, characteristics and thinking that make the difference in an organisational culture. How they think and act reflects the organisation.

"The purpose of an organisation is to benefit people and improve society," said the world's greatest entrepreneurial-minded corporate warrior. Referred to 'as an inspiration to people around the world,' by US president George Bush Senior, this unwell, uneducated, unknown and unlikely warrior, created the world's biggest company, helped his country's economic prosperity, started management practices now embraced by globally, founded what are now internationally recognised institutes for leadership and research, donated huge fortunes to worthy causes and served hundreds of millions of customers with innovative products that improved the quality of life. The list of his achievements is very long, as are the volumes that amount to the mini library he has written on business and human philosophy. Yet the message of Konosuke Matsushita to his organisation was short and simple: *"think like an entrepreneur, not a hired hand."*

For him, as an entrepreneur, he believed that the mission of management lay in satisfying the human instinct for improving the quality of life. Founding household names including Panasonic, Technics, and National, the Matsushita Electric Company of Japan created an entrepreneurial climate that was conducive to seeking opportunity, advancing innovation, developing leadership and giving service. Konosuke Matsushita considered his ultimate creation the organisation itself, because of what it stood for in developing people and serving society. There is no doubt that the entrepreneurial climate; characteristics and management teachings ultimately fostered the hundreds of thousands of entrepreneurs, innovators and leaders involved. Yet it was these people in return who were ultimately instrumental in developing one of the greatest entrepreneurial corporations of the 20th century.

> **The purpose of an organisation is to realise its potential.**
> **Realising its potential lies in the strength of its purpose.**

Similar to other great success stories that dramatically influenced the 20th century such as Ford, Citicorp, Sony and Pfizer, to name a few from four different industries, none achieved success in an upward direction. It was the volatile early part of that century that honed the entrepreneurial climate and characteristics that made them winning corporations. With the continuing economic globalisation, emerging competitive markets and increasing customer expectations the next few decades will be no less volatile, though with different conditions and challenges.

To ignore such a view is tantamount to a refusal to acknowledge the fact that history repeats itself. In the speed of thought economy over the next 50 years, customer is king and best practice will be measured by deed, not word. Those organisations that do not move with agility will fall over themselves. The leaders who do not develop others will have no followers.

The executive who does not think like an entrepreneur will lose. The real winners will serve their businesses, clients, customers and communities while living the core values of the company that they have chosen to be part of. Like the warriors of economic history he or she will be willing to fight for a worthwhile purpose greater than themselves

Credo & spirit v Re-engineering

Business is, and will remain as, the great modern arena for individuals to express their vocation and develop potential. Strengths and talents will always be best cultivated in the framework of a worthwhile organisational purpose. Ideally, when a company starts out it focuses on why it has been formed, where it wants to go, how will it get there and what it needs to do so. It utilises its strengths and talents to grow without concern about competition.

Clearly, this ideal is not always the case. J. Willard Marriott did not set out to go into the hotel business. He had a desire to go into business but as to which type he had no idea. Messrs. Hewlett and Packard started a company that developed anything that people would buy, even an electric shock machine to induce weight loss. The founder of Nordstrom started a shoe shop for something to do. Today, even though their founders are no longer around, these companies lead their industries. All three have core ideologies, however, that are set in stone. Would the companies be where they are without the evolution of a credo to guide them? Maybe. Certainly they would not have developed to the heights of influence that they did. But, more importantly, would they have ever come into being without the spirit of entrepreneurship? The answer is no. Ask yourself. Would any of the organisations that you have been involved with have come to life without the existence, or influence of, an entrepreneurial spirit?

Such spirit, or courage when coupled together with a credo, or raison d'etre, seems to be the vital ingredients that are fundamental to building great corporations, partnerships and institutions that last. The reality, however, for most established organisations is that such spirit or credo is ignored particularly when times are good. An impending crisis may cause a revisit to them, in the same way that all of us silently call for guidance when our world seems to be falling in, but usually crises are passed to legal departments.

When Perrier's bottled water was tampered with they did not take the same action that the medical organisation Johnson & Johnson took when they met with a similar crisis. Guided by their 'set in stone credo,' that begins with: *'our first responsibility is to the doctors, nurses, hospitals, mothers and all others who use our products'* immediately they knew of the threat that cyanide had been introduced to one of their products, Tylenol, Johnson & Johnson responded decisively. The threat seemed isolated to one city however, since the product was available throughout the US they removed all of it, at an estimated cost of $100 million. At the same time they mounted a mammoth communication program to advise the public. Public confidence in Johnson and Johnson never even faltered; moreover it was strengthened as the public viewed the company as one that always protected them regardless of cost.

Where Johnson & Johnson clearly responded, Perrier reacted. Though the threat related to a foreign body in the bottle that could induce cancer, Perrier appeared to the public to be playing down the seriousness of it. The public was told that even if you consumed an enormous amount of their product you would still be safe. The organisation withdrew the bottles from the affected areas and mounted a huge advertising campaign to indicate that Perrier was good for you. This did not bring back public confidence in the measure that was hoped for and many competing brands benefited. When it comes to anything life threatening, customers don't want words, they want action. The fact that a business's fortunes are dependant on its customers is, incredibly, forgotten by many organisations.

> **No organisation comes to life without the existence, or influence of, an entrepreneurial spirit**

Many organisations, similar to individuals, almost seem to become their own worst enemy. There is almost a correlation between, good times and plentiful budgets and a form of professional complacency. To the degree that an organisation takes for granted that it is a successful industry leader with many customers, and ahead of its competition, seems proportionate to its losing sight of its reason for being. In place it builds a picture that it is the issue. Complacently believing its own propaganda of how important and invincible it is; external focus diminishes from its original strengths of building relationships, delivering to customers and rewarding those who are involved. Inexorably a metamorphosis starts to happen.

The established 'professionally complacent' organisation starts insidiously changing from an entrepreneurially minded warrior culture to a hired-hand worrier culture. It becomes more concerned about its weaknesses and the strengths of its competitors. Seemingly still successful in spite of itself though, any reductions in anticipated returns are blamed on poor market conditions, changes in government legislation allowing unregulated newcomers in the industry, changes in interest rates or lack of good people in the recruitment market. As the organisation has also increasingly become more internally concerned on its weaknesses it is noticed that communication is poor, innovative thinking is non-existent and there is little team spirit.

This is not perceived as a problem because as times have been favourable for training budgets, re-engineering programmes can be bought in from the outside. They seem to work at first, changes happen but then once again the organisation unconsciously gravitates back to the more comfortable habit of worrying about what it can't do and waiting for the market and other conditions beyond its control to improve. Though it feels strong enough to weather any storm of difficult times, it believes it prudent to announce job cuts. After all it convinces itself, as the rationalising begins, even though the re-engineering programme was clear that people were the 'best asset,' it also advocated that they should be whittled down and the remainder honed up. Transformation is complete; the warrior has been reduced to a worrier.

It can be argued that there will be certain times that are so disastrous that 'laying off' the 'best asset' is the only option. During the stock market crash of 1929 millions of people became unemployed. No corporation was immune to the market changes that followed. Matsushita Electric had its sales drop by more than 60% and though 'laying off' seemed the only option, it was not taken. The company was determined not to throw its people into poverty. After all, part of its founding spirit and credo was to: *'relieve society from the misery of poverty and bring it wealth.*' Cutting production dramatically the company had their 'best asset' work for half-days in the factory and half-days doing their utmost to sell its backlog of inventory.

The warrior spirit of asking thousands of factory workers to be sales people is rarely considered today. If it were perhaps the UK would have more than just the one or two remaining British car manufacturers that turn out less than 3,000 cars a year between them. Creating ambassadors is common sense, though not common practice, and is covered in a later chapter. With everyone at Matsushita Electric working full time for the very survival of the company, the innovation worked within just three months. As regular shifts recommenced without the concern of increasing inventory, focus was put into new products to meet the changing markets. Though 'times were poor for training budgets,' recruitment and apprentice programs increased. What else could they do? They were an entrepreneurially-minded corporation.

Cultivating the Basics

No business is recession proof but organisations must accept that because markets do fluctuate their customers' ability to buy must be monitored. Otherwise, they are left very quickly with loads of stock for which there is no demand. With the 'sudden sharp economic downturn,' as the media proclaimed it, at the start of this century, High-Tech organisations that claimed to be customer-focused and agile were caught out. They tended to believe more in their technology than their own common sense and basic management principles. Cisco, the icon hailed by management gurus as the prototype corporation for the 21st century and best admired by both its people and customers alike showed how vulnerable it was to an economic downturn.

Though it expounded a strategy of forging alliances with its suppliers to eliminate inventory the downturn caught the company so unawares that it had to write off over $2billion in inventory. Though it had the latest electronic data to detect even the smallest market changes, it did not see the slide until too late and later announced a 99% reduction in profits. Not just Cisco, but its rivals in the telecom equipment market were caught out. Nortel announced one of the biggest quarterly losses ever recorded - $20billion – with thousands of 'lay-offs;' Uniphase announced year-end losses in excess of $50billion. Toshiba 'laid-off' over 18,000 of its 'best asset' after realising that its original profits forecast of Yen60billion would turn into a Yen115billion loss. Relying too much on their forecasting systems they failed to do basic homework. The customer orders information that was relied upon to measure demand was still providing double, triple and in some cases quadruple figures formerly entered to overcome previous scarcity. The information provided by state of the art technology may be the best available; but it can only ever be as good as an organisation's interpretation of it.

As organisations become somewhat blinkered and influenced by too much success, rather than motivated by basic principles, the bottom line will always suffer. And when the bottom line suffers it is because of the top line forgetting to apply basics. There are certain questions that all leaders should regular ask, and answer, in order to remind themselves of the basics. For the fact of the matter is that business is simple. As success grows we complicate it. Business today too often illustrates Man's ability to complicate simplicity.

When I built my first business in residential property I followed basic principles that I had learned from being raised on a small farm in Scotland. Choose your field, prepare the ground, plant at the right time, nurture your produce, reap when ripe, reward and thank any help you received as well as your customers for being regular, reinvest profit in more seed, maybe for some additional land and also for hard times that may suddenly arise in the future, and finally inspect your field. Simple, but if not followed there is no money or food. With no food you don't eat. As human beings we need to eat or die. Similarly if a business is not fuelled, then, quite simply, it fails.

Clearly as everything in nature is an undeniable state of evolution it is the nature of Mankind to grow. As Man is subject to natural laws it follows that any expression from Man is under the same influence. Applied to business, this means that even though products and industries will always come to the end of their usefulness, leaders must never forget that the natural direction for business is toward growth and development.

**Business processes illustrate clearly
Man's ability to complicate simplicity**

In farming, if there is a problem, you go to the root of the cause. If the seed does not grow, it is not the fault of the seed. It is the fault of badly prepared ground giving a lack of nutrients. If a young plant does not grow, it is not the fault of the plant; it is because of lack of sustenance and general nurturing. The strategy of pulling the plant out of the soil to check on progress will destroy it. These are basic natural flowing principles of life that put things in order when followed.

Though the word organisation comes from the word organise, to put things in order; and the place where products are created is called a plant, it is clear that with some organisations the comparison stops. Just imagine shareholders metaphorically pulling your plants out of the ground and warning them that if they do not grow faster they will not give them any more water. It is essential that leadership and management do not get bogged down in the minutiae of business. They must regularly revisit the basics by asking sequential questions as illustrated under organisational farming in Table 1.1.

In revisiting such basics, leadership can literally start sowing the seeds of greatness that will recreate them as an entrepreneurial corporation. Similar to the fact that too many relationships fall apart because they forget what brought them together; too many businesses fail because they lose sight of such basics. This makes perfect sense but the reality of it can be a different story. *Building* my first business was different to actually *managing* it. Success brings a different perspective to life and the basics are 'blinkered out' at our peril.

Basic Farming	Organisational Farming	Business Jargon	
1. Choose your field.	Why will this company exist?	Mission	L
2. Prepare the ground.	What are we about?	Values	E
3. Plant at the right time.	Where do we want to go?	Objectives	A
4. Nurture your produce.	What do we have?	Strengths	D
5. Ensure regular irrigation.	How will we get there?	Strategy	E
6. Reap when ripe.	Are our products developed?	Marketing	R
7. Bring to Consumer.	How well are they received	Revenue	S
8. Reward & Thank.	Do we deliver & follow through?	Service	H
9. Save & Invest Profit.	How are we going to expand?	Results	I
10. Inspect your field.	Is our process working?	Manage	P

Table 1.1

One of my first companies, Paramount Homes, was an early forerunner of luxury properties that were built to cater for the customer requirements. Though accepted today, at the time such development was unheard of. Within the architecturally designed residence the customer could choose the bathroom, kitchen and fittings that they wanted. The company's vision of *'providing homes to serve lifestyles'* began to become a reality.

Utterly focused on the customer, finding the right sites, and delivering to order, however, I lacked what I was later to learn were essential management skills. And although I surrounded myself with people whom I thought did have the necessary skills, I failed to recognise that they lacked them also. I became convinced by the figures that success had arrived and was here to stay. I had more money than I realised and I set about enjoying the trappings of newfound wealth. However, being a Scot even these were not excessive I hasten to add. What had been overlooked were the final two basics referred to above. Indeed non-adherence to these last, but by no means least, of the basics is very often found to be the reason for business failure. And failure can happen despite the size of the business.

Regardless of the size of investment, the basics are constant. And as all forms of speculative investment, which is the most common type that a business is involved in, inherently carries risk, it is even more important that the basics are adhered to. If not, financial folly follows. I labour the point because, incredible though it may seem, everyday the press carries stories of exploits that have clearly been externally influenced by hype, rather than internally driven by basics.

Though the principle of DotCom may be sound and 'customer convenient' with what appear to be low overheads, investment in them was often more due to following hype than following basics. Scot or not, who would want to invest in a business that although valued at hundreds of millions of dollars had the turnover of a corner shop without owning the premises? DotCom in 'farming' terms would mean ploughing up the White House gardens with the latest machinery in the hope that the seed would grow quicker and everyone would want to eat the fruits.

The 'farming' follies of the DotComs pales into insignificance, however, in comparison with the losses incurred by the TeleComs. By desperately seeking to outbid each other for third generation licenses in the fear that they may lose out, giant TeleComs bought to an end a 50 month period that had witnessed a $4 trillion investment rush for gold that was not there. The price was not determined by following the basics, nor was it being entrepreneurial, nor was it adhering to core values. To the later chagrin of shareholders a winning bid price ensured that they owned a part of a heavily debt-ridden organisation. A greater suffering was experienced by hundreds of thousands of 'best assets.' The only delight was for waste corporations dealing with disposal of a trillion dollars of countless tons of scrapped inventory. The desperation to cater for the volume of transferring data and voice was so successful that if everyone on the planet used the telephone continuously for a year their transmissions could be catered for within a couple of hours.

Similar to a building site, a new license is a risk investment that can only be made to deliver revenue after further development investment and, of course, assuming future customers are interested. But the sixth principle of reaping when ripe was overshadowed by the massive advertising campaigns telling customers how their world would be different when they signed up. Delivery did not match promises.

The turn of this century witnessed giant telecom organis-ations requesting multi-billion dollar rights issues from their shareholders so as not to be declared insolvent. At one time the UK's British Telecom had $50bn in borrowing. Royal Dutch Telecom (KPN) in the Netherlands had similar challenges. France Telecom had 64bn euros of debt. These national business flagships of their respective countries had ignored many of the natural basics principles.

As is often the case, there is greater concern over manmade practices than natural principles: For example: does the stock market find us favourable and how will they influence our shareholders? Pity the poor organisation involved in an industry that is experiencing a slow down in the fast-changing markets somewhere in the globe, wakes up to a nightmare of finding its stock mercilessly marked down by some faceless ghost in another industry who has preferred to follow the recommendations of others. Pity the poor organisation also that is subjected to such lemming behaviour, whilst issuing a profit to be proud of then discovers that billions have been wiped off the companies value because the profit was less than first reported. As Nokia experienced when they announced 42% growth instead of the 47 % expected in quarter profits at the start of this millennium.

Such nightmares may always continue to affect corporations, both non-entrepreneurial and entrepreneurial, particularly as media today revels in alarmist stories that make for good copy and circulation. The more agile and vision motivated organisation, however, will be less effected than the more inflexible shareholder driven one.

For my part, though money had been put aside for new sites, none had been put by for 'hard times.' I had forgotten to ensure to have in place what I now refer to as a business buffer. Being the major shareholder, however, I was able to use such agility to best advantage. Waking up one Christmas Eve to discover that my own funding source had been taken to the cleaners by a developer, defaulting on his massive loan, certainly demanded flexibility.

Fortunately for me, although I was not able to continue in the short term because of cash flow (no buffer), I did have a good site bank. By disposing of these sites quickly, although admittedly at discounted prices, I was able to complete all my current commitments and in time move the business and its philosophy into a national building group.

Harnessing the Pioneering spirit

So, 'new economy' high tech giants may not have adequately anticipated the economic slide until too late and reacted with massive lay-offs, huge write-offs and alarming profit warnings. Is this simply indicative of entrepreneurial corporations? No. Is it indicative that management skills are lacking? Not necessarily, though certainly those farthest from the customer seem to get things the most wrong. A few more 'old economy' established organisations, than new economy ones, were able to anticipate the turndown in time.

Dupont, for example, in paying close attention to the behaviour of their ultimate consumers, noticed that orders were declining in many of the industries they operated in. They were not so concerned about the middle wholesale businesses that bought their paint, clothing, medical supplies, carpets or chemicals; but whether *end* users were actually using their products. If every wholesaler has warehouses of your paint from which people may regularly buy, but no one is doing any painting then it will be not long before there will be huge surplus of inventory. By responding to the signals early, Dupont minimised both layoffs and write-offs.

The point here is not about being entrepreneurial or applying management skills or adherence to the basics. Leadership in organisations today must have *all three* of these elements. Because they each complement the strengths of the other two, operating best when harnessed. A pioneering or warrior spirit within a business context involves both the courage and experience to break new ground a the courage to go beyond prejudices and boundaries and seek out what is required to recreate the all-important spirit of entrepreneurship and the experience to be able to implement so that it works.

A new type of leadership is not what is required; the rekindling of an authentic one, however, is. A leadership that releases people's potential while stimulating the spirit of entrepreneurship is required; *entrepreneurial* leadership.Though the sound theory that developing leadership attributes throughout an organisation will release potential is generally accepted today, in practice it has not been entirely successful. Since developing entrepreneurial behaviour is going to become accepted as the key to organisational success, it is more important than ever that leadership works.

In *The Eureka Principle*, I sought to clarify authentic leadership, by blending eastern philosophy with contemporary western experience. Here my conviction is that corporate entrepreneurship is critical for future and sustained business growth. Therefore, it is important to make clear what organisations must do to ensure that leadership fosters entrepreneurial behaviour. First, however, I will explain why the leadership of many organisations either wittingly or unwittingly does not get the best out of their people, particularly in relation to creating entrepreneurial spirit.

In most organisations 'Leaders' are actually managers operating under a leadership title, Table 1.2, refers to them as m-leaders. M-leaders knock the pioneering spirit out of their people; mostly unwittingly, but sometimes on purpose. This is because of either hidden agendas or sticking to the misguided habit of: 'Do unto others what you have had done unto you.' Though everyone may be born with qualities of leadership there will always be differing levels of different strengths applicable to different situations within different individuals. As the root of education means to bring out what is within, it is the responsibility of teachers and parents, while we are young, to bring out the best in children.

1. m-leaders knock the pioneering spirit out of their people.
2. m-leaders give little or no responsibility.
3. m-leaders are not role models for entrepreneurship.
4. m-leaders allow slow decisions to extinguish creativity.
5. m-leaders perceive entrepreneurs to be rash risk-takers.
6. m-leaders allow operational efficiency to have priority over innovation.
7. m-leaders dominate with blame more than stimulate with praise.
8. m-leaders are more interested in their own entrepreneurial development.
9. m-leaders communicate only when they want something.
10. m-leaders do not like change because they are already too busy.

Table 1.2

Generally there are no bad pupils, just bad teachers. Starting without inhibitions each of us naturally display our strengths to varying degrees. Displaying too much of a quality, though, can often lead to its discouragement through cautionary advice, however well intended. We learn quickly as children that it is often easier to go along than get along. Conditioned habits of 'discouraging' grow until the day comes when we do the very same things to others.

Leadership is about encouraging the spirit of others. Anytime a 'leader' does the opposite involves unclear motives or hidden agendas. Such a leader is in name only. Knowing how to be a leader is not the same as acting as one. The same applies to the organisation. Calling itself a 'learning' one is not the same as being one, though it may be a start towards becoming one. Now, more than any time in history, a burden of responsibility rests on organisations to educate, stretch and challenge their people continuously. Certainly more of a person's life is spent at work than at school.

But let us not forget that the real responsibility lies with the individual. Unless there is both a passion and a discipline to develop through lifelong learning, in all its possibilities; and a commitment to share with others such learning and experience in order to bring out the best in them, helping them to surpass us in what they achieve, how can we call ourselves leaders?

Leadership is about encouraging the spirit of others and can never involve hidden agendas.

Dampening down enthusiasm or holding back an initiative because it is going too fast for us, and we need time to think how it may affect us, impedes progress. But, you may argue, what if experience highlights that if we do not hold back, failure will be certain? Mistakes are the best measure of progress and growth. Certainly we learn more. If a leader has not made mistakes, will he or she have had the opportunity to learn? More alarmingly will they have developed the courage to make big decisions? No. If the future demands more entrepreneurial groundbreaking organisations, then future leaders must ensure that they encourage others to develop their pioneering spirit.

Executives who aspire to be such leaders must ask what level of responsibility they allow.

Do they currently have the authority of the chairman when dealing with every customer?

If they don't will they allow the same low level of responsibility with their own people?

If they want to show how their fellow employees can be entrepreneurs how good a role model are they?

Are they able to make quick decisions when innovation demands it?

How do they perceive entrepreneurs?

Are they loose cannons that will eat up whole budgets with crazy notions?

Is the efficiency of their operation more important to them than innovations that demand system changes?

Do they take the time to praise regularly, or are they content to just appraise when required?

If entrepreneurial development means great entrepreneur reward are they more interested in their own development than their employees who are also keen?

Do they communicate only when they want something done or when something has gone wrong?

Do they support change while not being part of it?

The answer will always be communicated to others. Communication is more than words, and leadership is easier done than said and harder to define than recognise. Yet when people see it they know it and follow.

The role of an entrepreneurial leader, which for the purposes of Table 1.3 I have referred to as an e-leader, is not necessarily to be an entrepreneur. Neither is it to seek out opportunities, new innovations, utilise competitive insights, make the best of uncertainty nor have the agility of cat. It is far greater. It is to be part of the dynamic responsible for creating an corporation that encourages all of its people to learn, develop and apply these qualities by acting in an entrepreneurial way.

> **Leadership is easier done than said**
> **Harder to define than recognise**
> **Yet when people see it they know it.**

Learning to become an entrepreneurial leader involves authenticity: behaving as a real leader in action, rather than simply in title. Such real leadership echoes the immutable principle taught throughout history: Lead from the front. How is it possible to encourage people to go beyond if you are managing them from the rear? The finest warriors in history led from the front. Alexander did not build scores of cities by himself. Matsushita did not build scores of businesses by himself. But their behaviour and action was certainly instrumental.

Executives committed to being authentic leaders must ask if they genuinely encourage their people to take initiatives and go much further than might be expected of them when dealing with a request from a customer, a brief from a client, or when supporting a colleague. They must ask if they always look beyond the horizon themselves.

With increasing uncertainty and unpredictability part and parcel of our business world; where an overlooked opportunity jumped on by a competitor can change a market; how can conventional structure and systems managed by a rearguard be applicable today? Management must have confidence to act on and expect others to use their initiative in the knowledge that they are following and expected to duplicate the actions of a real leader. In which case the executive, committed to being a real leader, expressly gives confidence to others to act on initiative. And, in doing so, they naturally foster entrepreneurship through example.

1. e-leaders encourage their people to go beyond the brief
2. e-leaders give confidence to act on initiative
3. e-leaders foster entrepreneurship through example
4. e-leaders don't allow structure to stymie creativity
5. e-leaders perceive entrepreneurs to be purposeful initiators
6. e-leaders give innovation priority over operational efficiency
7. e-leaders forgive rather than insist on permission
8. e-leaders are interested in everyone's entrepreneurial development
9. e-leaders communicate by listening attentively
10. e-leaders embrace change all the time

Table 1.3

As creativity is the key to new business development, closer customer relationships and exciting innovations to market, the authentic leader will ensure that structure is not restrictive. Structure in an entrepreneurial organisation is flexible. The backbone with its network of essential services is best when it is agile. High-rise buildings in earthquake sensitive areas must have built in flexibility or crumble when their very foundations are hit by change. Rigid structures favoured by control-centric management will ultimately be insecure.

An e-leader forgives rather than insists on permission. If the engineer, Charles House, had not ignored David Packard's order to stop working on a current project he believed in, the high-quality monitor used in manned moon landings and countless surgical operations would not have been completed and HP would never have received the millions of dollars in revenue that it did. If Steven Wozniak had been allowed to act on his initiative, perhaps HP would have developed the first personal computer. Today that organisation is interested in everyone's entrepreneurial development and they certainly listen more attentively.

Redefining Management

The latter part of the 20th century witnessed an abundance of management training. Moving away from a hierarchal decision making process towards a flatter more fluid organisation was viewed as the way to enter the promised land of effectiveness and future success. The motives were right. But was it successful? Behaviour and reward when strongly linked are the basis of a corporate culture.

When a managers' rewards in both remuneration and recognition is reliant on their fulfilling a responsibility to maintain a controlled structure in which people follow instructions given, and perform them without error, they are *not* going to change behaviour.

If change involves any diminishment of reward, behaviour will fight against it. Training a manager to be a professional manager, therefore, simply provided some great psychological techniques to exert control. The outcome today is that whichever way you cut it the majority of organisations remains hierarchal in both process and thinking, even if the structure is seemingly flatter.

Having invested in a change-management process one particular organisation, that perceived itself to be no longer hierarchal, insidiously succumbed to pressure from managers as it expanded. Pleased with itself for having reduced its decision process from six to just two signatures, it unwittingly increased them to seven within as many months. Certain 'excluded' managers feeling that their authority had been usurped made it their goal to become an essential part of the established process as a measure of their position. Authority and status was put ahead of speed and creativity. Very quickly the organisation returned to the former state it occupied prior to any change process.

Management is essential for business; as leadership is; as entrepreneurship is. But the elements do involve different thought processes, different agendas and different outcomes. Leadership, however, is the common denominator for both successful management and successful entrepreneurship. But, in the same way that people choosing to diet will revert to their particular body type when they stop, they will, after immersing themselves in leadership training, often revert to habitual thinking.

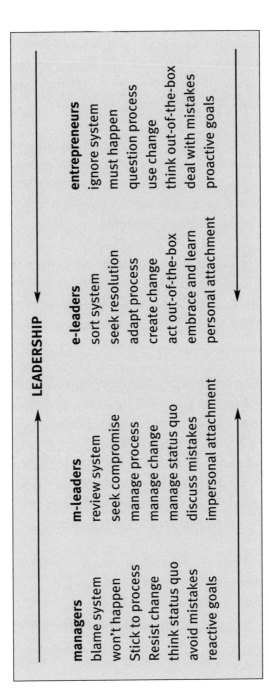

LEADERSHIP

managers	m-leaders	e-leaders	entrepreneurs
blame system	review system	sort system	ignore system
won't happen	seek compromise	seek resolution	must happen
Stick to process	manage process	adapt process	question process
Resist change	manage change	create change	use change
think status quo	manage status quo	act out-of-the-box	think out-of-the-box
avoid mistakes	discuss mistakes	embrace and learn	deal with mistakes
reactive goals	impersonal attachment	personal attachment	proactive goals

Table 1.4

Until leadership is embraced as a lifelong learning process that challenges and tests this will always be the case. The simplest views of m-leaders and e-leaders illustrated in Table 1.4 highlight the differing agendas.

A traditional management perspective has influenced an m-leader; an entrepreneurial perspective has influenced an e-leader. The clearest difference is that the latter is more likely to view the world in 'ownership' terms; while the former will view the world in 'doing a job' terms.

The major requirement for developing organisations is to instil a sense of 'ownership,' particularly at 'leadership' level. But with change actually being harder to achieve at the top in every organisation, instilling such ownership has always been a challenge.

It may not be required in smaller ventures that do not have large numbers of people and few levels of hierarchy, but a redefinition of management is required in larger corporations. Conventional management will hold an impersonal view towards goals and certainly will not have the tendency to feel passionate about them. They are simply a means to getting their job done. Words to win hearts and minds may be spoken, but their intention is in getting the job done.

Language of change without the action is not the basis of real leadership. And managers today must be leaders to fulfil their role effectively. Such people should have a desire to be authentic leaders, be decisive in their actions and be ambitious for the corporation's interest, not their own. Because being ambitious for the company's interest ensures that the *right* communications are *always clearly* sent throughout the command chain – an important objective business still struggle with.

> **The impersonal view of conventional management does not motivate a passion towards goals.**

Management's first responsibility should be to ensure the right things are done because they want to be done, not because they have to be done. This is in line with ensuring that an organisational strategy is internalised by all. The difficulty with the title of manager today is that it can mean controller, administrator and leader. Yet all these elements involve different agendas. Certainly, the first two are not conducive to creating an entrepreneurial corporation. A controller will tend to hold back; an administrator will tend to tie down; a leader will guide forward. Those managers that do have a tendency to leadership will have displayed certain characteristics during their formative years – heading up teams at schools for example. They will be the ones that when 'laid-off' they take the opportunity to develop their own business. These leading-managers are already 'taking-ownership' minded. Those managers that lean towards controlling will often go to work in the leading-managers new business. If, striving to remain consistent with what they are most familiar with, these controlling-managers seek to maintain status quo, then the leading-manager's ideas may be held back.

Choosing management within organisations today still follows certain routes that do not adhere to common sense. Too often it is used as a tool for promotion or recognition.

People who have absolutely excelled in their specialist field because of certain strengths, for example, are often 'promoted' to a management position that will bring to bear their weaknesses. The result is that you have lost a specialist and gained bad management. Recognition and promotion should be specifically endowed as appropriate.

Another common route to management is to gain a degree or MBA. Both are important but they are more effective when they are viewed as the beginning of management development and not the end of it. Too often the perception is that after achieving such a level of education they are ready to go forth and prosper. Far from it, as a leader's first responsibility is be a lifelong student of both people and their specialist subject. How can management manage the development of others if they stop managing their own personal development?

The common sense route for effective management today must involve being yourself and doing what comes naturally. Management must be redefined and re-routed from one of viewing people as simply resources to control, to one of taking ownership for organisational success.

Defining Entrepreneurship

For many years I have been fascinated at the different thinking between employee-ship and ownership. During my 30 years in business I have experienced being an apprentice, employee, employer, manager and board director. I have also experienced being an entrepreneur, a partner and an owner of an organisation. My research has persistently interacted with and studied for the criterion that makes a person become an employee, employer, manager, entrepreneur, even real leader, and what makes one person want to achieve, serve and innovate more than a colleague, relative or partner. It is therefore my conviction that the route to instilling this important sense of ownership is through understanding, developing and forming entrepreneurial characteristics, as they are very the very foundation of real leadership.

The traditional route from graduate/trainee to manager, and now to professionally trained m-leader is taken, for the majority, with an employee mind-set. Unfortunately, this route too often beats the entrepreneurial spirit out of employees or, at the very least, trains it out of them. The alternative route from entrepreneur to e-leader involves a more confident mindset. How to evolve from employee to entrepreneur in order to capitalise on the characteristics and performance essential in creating entrepreneurial organisations is explained in chapter two. First it is important to make certain definitions.

1. Entrepreneur is a French word literally translated as between-taker. Perhaps the earliest example of a between-taker, or someone who takes risks and starts something new was Marco Polo. He contracted with European merchants to sell their products in the east. He sought opportunity out and capitalised on it for the benefit of all stakeholders.

His personal investment of enormous amounts of energy, time and risk paid dividends in opening up the known world's first communication link reflected real global behaviour! Unwittingly by placing meat under the saddles of horses to grind tender ready to be put between bread, Polo was in part instrumental in developing the hamburger. So, clearly, he was an energetic innovator with an eye on future trends and customer focused. Perhaps his rugged style was even a forerunner of Ralph Lauren!

To define simply therefore: an entrepreneur is a creative innovator who acting on initiative, seeks and maximises opportunity, takes the required risk, and energetically rides it to a worthwhile conclusion. It is important to clarify 'worthwhile' because monetary or profitable objectives are not the main concern of an entrepreneur. It is the passion of what they believe in that motivates them to action. Successful non-profit making organisations, institutes and schools, are so because of an entrepreneurial spirit driving them.

2. Entrepreneurship involves more than an individual. It involves the whole team engaging in a process of willingly working together, risking creating, implementing, driving and following through an innovative idea that delivers measurable value. Within organisations this involves an approach to management that seeks to maximise value from opportunity without constraint to existing models, structure or resources.

Understanding of entrepreneurship as a group activity must not be at the expense of suppressing individual entrepreneurial behaviour. Overcoming such barriers requires adjustments in the actual way organisations are structured. How this can be addressed is discussed in Part 3. For the moment, and in the corporate context intended, to be successful all team members must embrace entrepreneurship. A shift in context can impact a corporation from bad to good with entrepreneurship. For example because of the Tylenol incident referred to earlier, a badly performing packaging company was able to utilise its tamper proof seals beneficially, resulting in a dynamic shift in its fortunes. When a team works together it heightens the awareness to notice the 'right' worthwhile opportunities to capitalise on.

3. Entrepreneurial Organisations promote entrepreneurial activity adapting structure, management and processes accordingly in order to gain the required agility, speed, creativity and drive to profitably act upon specific opportunities. In doing so they are able to cultivate an entrepreneurial culture that harnesses the benefits of uncertainty and risk oriented endeavours; be aggressive in winning business in the competitive arena, be proactive in developing innovative products and building market relations; and to generate significant return and value disproportionate to their resources.

To engage upon such a transformation for a bureaucratic established organisation can be likened to turning an oil tanker into a challenge cup competing yacht. Such a task requires both energy and courage yet must be embarked upon for the reasons stated within this opening chapter. Examples of successful organisations that have, or are engaging upon, transforming to entrepreneurial corporations are referred to in Part 2. All have recognised the importance of following the route that the fourth definition involves.

4. Entrepreneurial Leadership involves instilling the confidence to think, behave and act with entrepreneurship in the interests of fully realising the intended purpose of the organisation to the beneficial growth of all stakeholders involved.

Jack Welch of GE; Michael Dell of Dell; Konosuke Matsushita of Matsushita Electric; Richard Branson of Virgin; Masaru Ibuka of Sony; and a host of other 'lifetime' servants to their organisations could illustrate entrepreneurial leadership. But what they achieved or the characteristics they display is not the issue here. Re-creating an entrepreneurial organisation is not about the individual. If it were, these organisations would discontinue after the individual has gone. It is about developing an overriding influence conducive to releasing the potential and entrepreneurship of its 'best assets.'

Forming the characteristics of entrepreneurship and developing entrepreneurial leadership attributes at every level of the organisation is clearly the key to recreating those organisations that owe their very origin and growth to such spirit. It is not so much about reinventing as rediscovering and re-implementing those vital ingredients that will guarantee their future success. My role is not so much to convince established organisations of the need to become more entrepreneurial, as explaining *how* they can become more entrepreneurial. Teaching is more effective when the student is willing, and returning from conditioned worrier to natural warrior is a campaign that requires agreement. The first challenge is to move from employee-minded to entrepreneur-minded.

Entrepreneur is a creative innovator who acting on initiative, seeks and maximises opportunity, takes the required risk, and energetically drives it to a worthwhile conclusion.

Entrepreneurship is willingly working together, risking, creating, implementing, driving and following through an innovative idea together that seeks to maximise value from opportunity without constraint to existing models, structure or resources.

Entrepreneurial Organisations promote entrepreneurial activity adapting structure, management and processes accordingly in order to gain the required agility, speed, creativity and drive to profitably act upon specific opportunities.

Entrepreneurial Leadership involves instilling the confidence to think, behave and act with entrepreneurship in the interests of fully realizing the intended purpose of the organisation to the beneficial growth of all stakeholders involved.

Table 1.5

Chapter 2
Evolving Employeeship
Entrepreneurship

DO YOU REMEMBER YOUR FIRST TIME? The nerves, the anticipation, the excitement. All the questions you asked of yourself. How will it be for me? What will be expected of me? Will it be obvious that it is my first time? How long will it take? How will I perform? What will be the outcome? Should I take notes?

Few people remember their first ever business meeting because as the years pass they become as countless as conference handshakes. Take a moment to reflect on the meetings you have attended in the last few months. Were you fully prepared for each meeting? Did they have a fruitful outcome? Did you suggest that you would deal with something? Have you followed through yet with what you agreed to? Did you arrange to have another meeting? How did you behave? Were you proactive or reactive? Were you passive or contributory? If you had to categorise yourself as one or the other, would you say that you were a warrior or are worrier?

Why do we have meetings? Is that what business is about? I often ask such questions when attending conferences. Business is about solving problems, a CEO will tell me.

Business is about making a profit, another will answer. It's about keeping the plates spinning, a third may remark. Others offer: making the most of opportunity; focusing on new development; keeping the customer happy; keeping the shareholders happy; and even earning a living. Some executives have various suggestions from fire fighting to task focusing; recruiting good people to resolving disputes. Seeing the business world from their particular perspective, one of course might argue that all responses are right one way or another. None of them, however, respond with: business is about meetings. Yet, when prompted, all admit that they are either frequently setting up or attending one. Many are also honest enough to add that most meetings have vague agendas, are ill prepared for, and are not expected to have a definitive outcome.

Clearly not all meetings are a waste of the millions of daily hours expended on them. Yet far too many are, particularly those in large established organisations. Highly qualified employees busy themselves with a series of back-to-back meetings, measuring their success by the quantity they attend. This is not what business is about and not what meetings are for. A meeting is too often inefficient with either unstructured discussion or little discussion because two members are engaged in dialogue while others passively listen, thinking about what they could otherwise be doing. Board meetings that may start out well soon comprise of bored members because of tedious protracted discussion. All too often time runs out before important topics are covered. And far too often, new business development projects, innovative ideas and creative alternative strategies are included in the 'any other business' section at the end of an agenda.

In my experience, of attending both board and 'bored' meetings 'any other business' can be the most useful from a business growth perspective. Is there indeed any other perspective for business? Would the financial services division of General Electric have grown from $250m to $250Bn if, under the entrepreneurial leadership of Gary Wendt, every meeting had not been focused on business growth? GE Leader, Jack Welch expected entrepreneurship from Gary Wendt, whom in turn expected entrepreneurship from every member of his division. Are expectations really able to have such an effect? Would the growth outcome have been different if the expectations had been low?

Yes, of course. Despite this, however, research undertaken at schools, which shows how well students respond to high expectations from teachers, does not influence the policy of measuring different low expectation criteria and implementing teaching methods as appropriate. Similarly, in many organisations, training on how to deal with customers is based on the 1% of difficult customers, rather than on the 99% of good customers. In researching what keeps relationships together emphasis is placed on resolving past expectations that led to break up, rather than on developing future expectations that bond.

Institutional psychology is more interested in the expectations that make people depressed, rather than in those that make them happy. Management expects to spend more time on why revenue is down, than why it is up; more time on errors than discussing ideas; priority over customer recording procedures than on developing customer relations.

Expectations are commonly based on what people are *not* good at, rather than on what they are good at. The regularity of the refrains: 'you can't do that' or 'what else did you expect' is indicative of an organisation's culture that expects employees to be just that – employee-minded. A culture is directly influenced by people's expectations. Business expectations can be directly compared to doing press-ups. If you expect to do twenty, you start straining at seventeen. If you expect to do thirty, you will begin to feel the strain at twenty-seven. In business it is always the last quarter of the financial year when everyone begins to feel the strain to meet budget expectations. If, on the other hand, budget expectations look as if they are going to be reached in an early quarter, then everyone compensates by relaxing, usually too much, in order that expectations are fulfilled.

Business involves meeting expectations. Business growth demands exceeding expectations. Meetings, therefore, should be about setting *high* expectations. Make a decision right now to ensure that the very next meeting you arrange or attend has a definite purpose, sets high expectations from all those involved, establishes ownership of action and follow through with a conclusive time period. Try placing 'any other business' at the top of the agenda. If any element of it is about new business development, discuss it. If any element of it is not, ignore it. Why? Because any other business that does not relate to new business development and is not already itemised on the agenda should already belong to someone for decision and action. If none of the above is possible then cancel your meeting because your time will be more productive doing real business.

Business involves meeting expectations
Success demands exceeding expectations
Meetings must set great expectations.

Back in the early 1970's, during the first of four market downturns that I went on to experience, the company I worked with increased the frequency and duration of internal business meetings. They achieved little, however, other than to provide comfort on numbers and the general feeling was to 'weather the storm.' I recall one meeting during which the original entrepreneur that had founded the business made a statement in exasperation. 'It seems that our success has made us complacent. A few years ago we had no time for meetings, now our lives revolve around them. Meetings make us worry and procrastinate! Action brought us success. Let's go back to work.'

One might argue that such an attitude is like sweeping problems under the metaphorical carpet – as they will only build up and one day return to choke you. The fact is that though the downturns may be cyclical, alarming media announcements and worried discussions in the corridors and meeting rooms only distract you. It is far better to concentrate on what you can do, than on worrying about things. At your next meeting be aware how the focus of attention is on the why something can't be done – you may even catch yourself being the culprit.

Decisive meetings are very valuable. Unfortunately many meetings are either wittingly, or unwittingly, a tool to delay making decisions. In my second downturn of the early

1980's I was too involved in taking action to notice it. Though at that time I was borrowing at 4% above the 17% MLR – a total rate of 21%! (Minimum Lending Rate imposed due to International Monetary Fund requirements). The Prime Minister at the time, Margaret Thatcher, had taken on the unions, manufacturing was on its knees and, just when everyone was certain that it couldn't get any worse, war was declared against Argentina over the Falklands. The media was beside itself with alarm calls and the topic of most meetings were crippling interest rates, conscription concern and will they bring back rationing. Yet, within 60 months came the most affluent period for the West since the Second World War.

Just a few years later, however, in the recession of the early 1990's with interest rates at just 10%, half what I had been used to ten years earlier, I was more concerned about attending meetings to get out of trouble. Fortunately, I was able to become aware that my focus of attention was in the wrong direction. But it sometimes takes getting into a corner to make you turn round because, with your back safe and firm against the wall, you can once more focus in the right direction.

The main point is that developing entrepreneurship empowers you to respond with initiative. The very nature of employeeship is, unfortunately, less oriented to taking initiative. This is because most organisations have not created the environment that expects such action. Yet the early 1990's, similar to other recessions, was a time when there was a major increase in entrepreneurial businesses being started. And who started them? The hordes of redundant employees acting on their own initiative. Imagine if they had been allowed to develop their dormant entrepreneurial potential while working in the role as an employee. Their organisations would have greatly benefited.

In the 2001 downturn with interest rates at less than 5%, their lowest for four decades, the most common meetings for business were crises, chaos or creditor ones. Concern over fluctuating rates, market changes will make no difference to fluctuating rates and market changes. Only the nature and expectations of the organisation will make the difference.

The conditioned nature of a worrier may hope for the best, but it expects the worst. Conversely, the true nature of the warrior may hope for glory, but it expects the best. Which nature would best serve a corporation? If it is the nature of employeeship to have low expectations and the nature of the entrepreneurship to set high expectations then the task can be nothing short of evolving the former into the latter.

Making a Strategic Decision

Creating an entrepreneurial organisation is a strategic decision and where strategy is concerned it must involve full agreement to support. Strategy is too often misunderstood as being an operational initiative worth trying and which might gain edge over the competition. The role of strategy is to establish an *organisational edge* that will bring greater value to both customer and corporation. Entrepreneurship is about establishing a definitive edge to do just that. Therefore, as such it qualifies as a strategic decision that demands full agreement and support at the highest level.

Many organisations today lack a clear strategy. Influenced more over the strengths of the competition than their own, they are more interested in imitating than strategising. Leaders and management that want to act strategically must develop the qualities of entrepreneurship. In this way they will be able to obtain the edge that will outperform competition and deliver the cutting edge that both they and their customers are seeking.

> **The strategy of entrepreneurship establishes the definitive edge that brings greater value to both customer and organisation.**

Though making the strategic decision to be an entrepreneurial organisation may happen overnight, becoming one does not. Furthermore, and similar to any change in thinking process, it must be continuously, supported, monitored and allowed to evolve and grow. The process of developing entrepreneurship is by far the most effective for ensuring both continuous personal development and professional alignment.

Diligence must be taken to ensure that as the full power of entrepreneurship is released it is purposefully channelled. This of course, is in line with cultivating the basics; you do not just let produce grow – you nurture it while keeping a watchful eye on conditions. The difficulty with culture is that it is like air. It may look clear but it can insidiously grow foggy, which is hazardous in blinding people to what surrounds them. The entrepreneurial organisation must work towards developing the qualities shown in Table 2.1 as a matter of course.

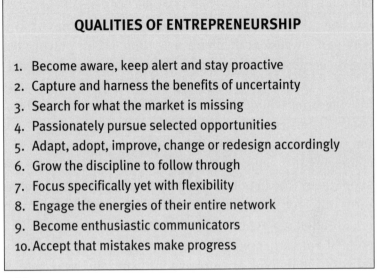

QUALITIES OF ENTREPRENEURSHIP

1. Become aware, keep alert and stay proactive
2. Capture and harness the benefits of uncertainty
3. Search for what the market is missing
4. Passionately pursue selected opportunities
5. Adapt, adopt, improve, change or redesign accordingly
6. Grow the discipline to follow through
7. Focus specifically yet with flexibility
8. Engage the energies of their entire network
9. Become enthusiastic communicators
10. Accept that mistakes make progress

Table 2.1

The starting point to ensure that such qualities become habitual is developing what I have identified as six core characteristics that both employees and organisations must develop contemporaneously. It is important for them to be developed together for the corporation to sustain corporate entrepreneurship. How they are to be developed will be explained further in Part 3.

The Six Core Characteristics

Most of the business world operates on a wing and prayer. That is why the majority of businesses continue to close within one year of starting, and too many organisations do not see read the signals of impending crises, excluding acts of God or terrorism of course. The good news is that although the percentage of closures has remained fairly constant, the standard set for operation has been raised. This is in part because of the implementation of best practice but mostly because customers have had enough of poor practice.

Moving from selling products to serving customers has been good for business because it has either embraced, or been forced to form, new habits in order to compete. Clearly, embracing new habits is more effective than being forced to adopt them. The important fact, however, is that such habits form the characteristics essential to fulfil both an organisation's potential and the individual's potential. As I pointed out earlier, what makes up the deciding personality traits of the individual entrepreneur is not the issue here. It is the characteristics of entrepreneurship that employees and organisations must develop as defined in the previous chapter.

Redefining management to create entrepreneurial organisations must involve a combination of recruiting the people that display entrepreneurial behaviour and training those employees who readily choose to take on the responsibilities that an entrepreneurial role demands.

1. Decisive Personal Choice together with Agreed Support Strategy

Without question these joint entrepreneurial characteristics are first and foremost. And their coupling together is vital. From the employee perspective being chosen is not the same as choosing. A person must *want* to fill a role. The most skilled warrior that has lost heart is of little use in a battle.

From the organisational perspective being told to support is not the same as supporting. I have often been asked to intervene when an initiative has been derailed because of manipulated support. Such support, defended as being in the interests of the company, is spawned from hidden agendas. Agreed support must derive from the highest level, be formulised into a strategy and then communicated throughout an organisation.

CORE ENTREPRENEURSHIP CHARACTERISTICS

Employee	Organisational
1. Decisive Personal Choice	Agreed Support Strategy
2. Design, Develop, Drive & Determine	Provide Initiative Sponsorship
3. Willingly risk moderate failure	Establish Trial & Error Metrics
4. Interdependent Member	Encourage Diversified Teams
5. Define Project Expectations	Allocate Venture Resources
6. Concept Value Recognition	Performance & Risk Reward

Table 2.2

This first point therefore reiterates the fundamental strategic decision that an organisation must make. Does it want to move towards being an entrepreneurial organisation? The answer can only be a yes or no because trying it out does not create the environment required for it to grow. Half-heartedness is a root cause responsible for failures in strategy with resulting cynicism and disillusionment in an organisation's direction and leadership. Imagine you are seeking reassurance for an impending appendix operation. 'Will it be alright?' You ask of your surgeon. 'Well,' he replies, 'a few of my colleagues and I don't really believe in the necessity of this operation these days and it will be a first for me. But I can see that something has to be done, so I'll give it a try.' Would you feel confident with that kind of support? No, of course not. Yet that is how many established organisations interpret providing support.

The organisation must engage in internal and external confidential surveys, in order to measure how entrepreneurial it is at the start. Impartial specialists at universities and business schools provide the most effective measured survey. Such assessments and surveys should be treated as useful guides to assist strategy and development. They will be useless if strategy and development remain uninfluenced.

For the employee there are three measuring tools that can assist in indicating entrepreneurial inclination and help towards making a decisive personal choice. Again such tools must be used to develop, not impede. The first is to answer a simple personal assessment as detailed in Table 2.3. The second is to engage in far more reflective personal mission workshop similar to the one illustrated in *The Eureka Principle* (alternatively this workshop document can be acquired freely through contacting the email address at the back of this book). Both these assessments should be completed without input from any other person and also without being shown to others. The reason for this is quite simple. There is the real *you* and there is the person you want others to think you are. Such self-evaluations are vital for continuous self-development and particularly for entrepreneurship.

QUICK ENTREPRENEURSHIP SELF-ASSESSMENT TABLE

Answer the following questions quickly and honestly choosing a number between 0 (low) and 10 (high).

1. How much do you like yourself? _____
2. How much do your colleagues like you? _____
3. How decisive are you? _____
4. How creative are you? _____
5. How effective are you? _____
6. How well do you take orders? _____
7. How good a leader are you? _____
8. How good a team member are you? _____
9. How well do you follow through? _____
10. How well do you overcome obstacles? _____
11. How responsible are you? _____
12. How well can you communicate? _____
13. How well do you take failure? _____
14. How well do you encourage others? _____
15. How much do you take ownership? _____
16. How well do you serve others? _____
17. How confident are you? _____
18. How lucky are you? _____
19. How risk oriented are you? _____
20. How well do you know yourself? _____

Table 2.3

The procedure of appraising and evaluating colleagues without first having personally appraised or evaluated ourselves is senseless. How can it be possible to effectively motivate others if we do not first know what motivates ourselves? We must be aware about being too judgemental in place of using good judgement.

The hardest element in completing the entrepreneurship self-assessment is to answer quickly and honestly. It is important, however, as it minimises the tendency of 'having second thoughts.' Life would be so much easier if we could only have second thoughts first as we could pay more attention to our intuition. If your scores total above 150 you are an excellent candidate for helping your organisation to become entrepreneurial. Moreover it is something that you willingly choose to do.

If your score is between 100 and 150 you are a good aspirant for wanting to develop entrepreneurship. If you scored between 50 and 100 you need to personally commit yourself to personal development that raises both your self-belief and confidence. Any score under 50 will require some serious personal and professional work on your part.

Knowing our own motives allows us to motivate others Not being judgemental allows us to apply good judgement.

The third assessment utilises the input of colleagues. It is to engage in a full 360-degree feedback analysed by a specialised computer program that guarantees confidentiality. As with the measurement of how entrepreneurial an organisation is, impartial specialists facilitating the process are the most effective. There are two vital factors to remember when engaging in a full 360-degree assessment. The first is to deliver the assessment with care, and the second is to allow time to discuss the feedback. These assessments can, and should, be very extensive and involve a lot of the candidate's time, thought and emotion. Dealing with results quickly and insensitively sends wrongs signals. The result is that rather than having increased self-awareness, it increases confusion and worry.

2. Design, Develop, Drive & Determine together with Initiative Sponsorship

Following hard on the heels of the ability to choose is the ability to create something tangible and of value. Entrepreneurship is not just about having an idea or seeing an opportunity. It is about having the confidence, or passion to develop it further and then drive it to a profitable conclusion. To allow such qualities to both come and work together in an initiative there must be genuine sponsorship. More importantly it must come from the highest level.

During my commission as external change agent for Pfizer UK, chairman and managing director, Ken Moran, proposed and sponsored the initiative. A true leader, he placed the initiative high on his agenda and instilled his colleagues with both the drive and determination to release potential in all areas. The sponsorship and involvement of all of Pfizer's country managers under the co-ordinated leadership of William Steer and Hank McKinnell at that time were certainly major factors in reaching the company's goal to be the world's number one healthcare organisation.

Clearly, consumers heard of their name following their development and launch of their drug relating to erectile dysfunction: Viagra. But prior to this almost all of us have benefited from their research and development. What mother has not applied the antiseptic TCP to their children? What doctor has not prescribed penicillin tablets? What good is a product without common focus and concerted leadership to bring it to market? It was entrepreneurial thinking that first founded Pfizer and continued entrepreneurship that allowed it to create real value from a drug that, though originally developed for another purpose, has been instrumental in improving the qualities of thousands of people's lives and relationships.

Asking the question why and then designing simple innovations to improve all areas of products, service, and process requires a belief in your natural creativity. To the degree that you use your creativity is relative to how creative you can be. Use it or lose it is the best adage for being creative.

Most corporations are desperate to develop their creative innovative edge, yet lack of genuine support results in them becoming their own worst enemy. It is a dire problem because increasingly the majority of a corporation's revenue comes from 'new innovative' products.

Creativity may certainly be at the heart of entrepreneurship, but it is not about being inventive or developing genius tendencies. Entrepreneurship involves the taking of an idea forward. Would we have ever been able to marvel at the achievements of General Electric if the 'inventive' Edison had not developed his ideas and driven them to become commercially viable?

The world is full of brilliant ideas that become useless simply because they are not acted on. Sadly, active mediocrity is more effective than inactive genius. Why? Because an average idea acted upon will be infinitely more successful than a great idea forgotten about.

> **Organisations become their own worst enemy when lack of genuine support prevents them developing a creative, ground-breaking edge.**

Entrepreneurship involves even more than this however. Many of us may admit to having designed, developed and driven a project. But the success of any idea, project, strategy or relationship will ultimately rest on how we determine it. I wholehearted believe that it is the *following through* of whatever we take ownership of that is the ultimate key to its success.

Sports coaches will nurture their protégées to persistently follow through; irrespective of how far ahead they are of the competition. The top golfer must follow through or cannot hit the perfect shot. Winning athletes must continue running after the line, or they will undoubtedly lose to competitors as they slow too soon.

Yet business will readily admit that when it comes to 'following through' they consistently fall down. The excuse of 'having too much to do' should never be acceptable as it is just an admission to being either unorganised or not prioritising. The key to follow through is developing persistence. How much we are prepared to persist is a measure of both our self-belief and what we are involved with; and it is the measure to gauge our progress in evolving from employeeship to entrepreneurship.

Organisations that are to provide sponsorship will do so more readily when initiatives are backed by persistence. As in the case of all six of these core entrepreneurial characteristics, though, it is important to reiterate that they work in unison. Organisations must be persistent in both their intention to develop entrepreneurship and their sponsoring of initiatives that come from it. Xerox will readily admit that if their thinking, particularly in respect to sponsorship, had been more entrepreneurial they would not have lost dormant entrepreneur employees such as Steve Jobs, founder of Apple Computers Inc. Learning from the experience, Xerox instigated a specific division to ensure initiatives have effective sponsorship. Though it has metaphorically developed an entrepreneurial 'challenger cup yacht', the parent corporation is still partly perceived as a somewhat bureaucratic oil tanker. It is moving, however, towards becoming an entrepreneurial organisation.

Taking metaphor to reality, the EasyJet airline, founded by Stelios Haji-Ioannou, was an initiative first sponsored by his family's oil tanker shipping line. The highly entrepreneurial, EasyGroup, is an organisation that covers car rental to Internet shopping and airlines to financial services. Applying the entrepreneurial characteristics of persistent 'follow through' together with sponsorship to his own shipping line, Stelios ensured that Stelmar Shipping was one of the best performing IPO's (initial public offering) for the year it went public in the US. Stelios an example of Entrepreneurial Leadership: blending the art of successful entrepreneurship with the science of organisational management that are reflected in his degrees of business acumen gained from the London School of Economics and City University Business School.

3. Willingly Risk Moderate Failure with Established Trial & Error Metrics

Our ability to persist develops our self-confidence to see things through and to overcome the inevitable obstacles that test us. Though risk is inherent within all opportunity, many corporations prefer to be risk adverse. This can only lead to missing opportunity. The very nature of success demands trial and error. Similar to all of us, every great innovator of the world had to learn to walk; any mistake attached to them was a measure for their progress. Carl Benz developed the internal combustion engine through trial and error. This automotive basis of vehicular travel did not happen overnight. Mercedes-Benz benefited from such willingness to risk failure.

Almost a century later it was in a Mercedes-Benz workshop that the diesel engineer, Burkhard Goschel developed his new concepts. This time the opportunities for such concepts were overlooked and instead provided the opportunity for Goschel to join BMW, a decision Mercedes Benz later regretted. Having penned the designs for both 3 and 5 series, being the creative genius behind the new mini, the Z3 sports roadster, the X5 and the C3 motorcycle, BMW have backed Goschel to develop the hydrogen-powered car. To do so the carmakers owners, the Quandt family, allocated a specific sum of 2Bn Euro Dollars. They could do this because of their success borne out of a previous failure, indeed their acquisition the British carmaker, Rover, almost bought BMW to its knees.

Extraction was painful and a strategic decision was taken to concentrate once more on its core business – producing premium cars. Utilising its experience to the full BMW established a budget for trial and error metrics associated with producing premium cars. BMW acknowledges that taking risks such as developing a hydrogen-powered car are part of developing opportunity. While no other carmakers believe that this is the way forward, BMW are investing in the entrepreneurship of Dr Goschel and his proven team. Trial and error metrics involve establishing the level of funding and time period required.

This may have to be adapted but it is important to galvanise an objective with both measurable resources and market launch dates. This is what I mean by moderating the risk. Putting 'good money after bad' and expending further time and energy on something to get out of it is not good practice. Entrepreneurship is about seeking the opportunity out of the adversity and driving forward in an alternative direction guided by measurable metrics. It is not about reversing backwards to minimise risk and counting the cost to maximise blame.

4. Interdependent Members within Encouraged Diversified Teams

An obstacle to overcome when commissioned to assist BT's Global Business Markets Operations (GBMO) to develop a customer service strategy was the resistance to creating diversified teams. Traditional organisational practices are not conducive to creating teams made up from different, even competing, units or divisions. It is considered that all members of a marketing team must be involved in marketing; a sales team should comprise of sales people; an engineering team involves engineers; audit or legal should comprise of accountants and lawyers respectively and so on. Each team within their division will usually build an insulating barrier around themselves to prevent penetration from other divisions. My argument that all divisions must work together where the customer is concerned was initially resisted on the basis that GBMO customers were of a magnitude that demanded different divisional expertise at different times.

When it was proven that lack of liaison between divisions was neither adding value to the customers nor saving costs for the organisation the next obstacle was persuading insular teams to work together. Incidentally the very word *di*vision, from divide or split up, is hardly conducive to developing common purpose. Corporations comprised of different divisions always have internal communication challenges when it comes to 'working together towards shared vision.'

Diplomacy was required by chosen entrepreneurial sponsors to assure divisions that it was not the intention to either usurp or diminish authority. Rather the objective was to create an entrepreneurial team, which due to the very nature of its members diverse thinking, could consider new opportunities for service to clients.

The success of these 'teams' stems from the frank open discussion, that is a natural element of them, and their ability to look at the same issues from different perspectives. Each member brings strengths that compliment those of the others generating an interdependence that crosses divisional boundaries. It is essential that these multidiscipline teams with their diversity of thinking receive full encouragement from their organisations. For it's the outcome for their diverse thinking that will enable the organisation to understand, and respond more effectively to, both customers and market opportunities. This, in turn, facilitates quicker dissemination and communication of lessons learned from both successes and failures to solve problems in a way that has not been done before. All this is conducive to creating a more entrepreneurial, agile and boundary-less culture.

Part of the encouragement must include choosing either a team leader, or nominated sponsor, that has the skills to diplomatically smooth paths thus ensuring that this boundary-less team develops, thinks and acts entrepreneurially. On this final point, to be successful every person chosen, and who chooses to be a member of such a diversified team, must understand and adopt what is expected of entrepreneurship.

5. Define Project Expectations with Allocated Venture Resources

This is not an easy entrepreneurial characteristic for an corporation to develop because of the formal built-in constraints with regard to budget and talent allocation and long-term commitments. For that reason it is important that the project has a clearly defined strategy and expectations.

Any new project to be embarked upon must first qualify by being consistent with a company's reason for being.

Two of the qualities I listed earlier in Table 2.1 were: *search for what the market is missing* and *passionately pursue selected opportunities.* Therefore, the decision to pursue an opportunity or project must only be taken if the venture that will result from that decision is in the interests of the business that will be supplying the initial resources to allow the venture to get off the ground. In addition, the venture must clearly be aiming to produce a product or service that will meet a demand that exists within a defined market – and that market must be such that it is able and willing to pay for a service or product that meets its needs.

Pursuing an opportunity must clearly be selected as a venture that is in the interests of the business that will have to commit initial resources to it, as well as clearly meeting a demand in a market that is willing to ultimately pay for it. The questions to be asked are:

Answers to these can ascertain how long market demand is likely to be; whether it will be short or long. Life Science organisations such as Monsanto look to the long-term because of the very nature of their genetic research in cereal production. Whereas Kellogg, the cereal supplier to supermarkets will look to the medium term and Wall-Mart will look to the short-term.

The customer ultimately dictates – and it will be interesting to learn how the customer votes on a new breakfast cereal for hangovers that at the time of writing is being tested.

Pharmaceutical organisations have their markets dictated by licence periods. Both technological corporations and manufacturers will increasingly have to educate customers as to how and why using their new technology will provide benefit. Customers themselves will always continue to buy products and services on the basis of how they perceive the benefit they will get from such a purchase. Dyson cut deeply into the established Hoover market not because customers wanted cleaner cleaners that cleaned more effectively. But because they perceived that a Dyson made housework less tedious.

The size of the market will directly influence the level and quality of resources. Percentage of revenue should be considered as well as actual market. If an organisation has just a small percentage of what is already a multi-billion dollar industry then any entrepreneurial venture that is going to increase market share will find it easier to attract resource commitment.

In larger markets there are three avenues to ensure resource allocation. One is to create a structure where a percentage of an individual's time can be devoted to pursue independent projects. 3M are an example of this where 15% of employee's time can be spent on such projects without questions asked. A second is to develop a large specific venture fund for independent projects. Shell is an example of this. And indeed organisations are increasingly following suit by placing sums of between $10m and $40m in 'venture business units.' Some are doing so because they have made the all important strategic decision to become entrepreneurial. Others are merely imitating their competitors at the moment – but at least some action in the right direction is better than no action, though if the sums are not used for entrepreneurial ventures it seems a little pointless.

The third goes further by creating a separate entrepreneurial venture company that can be spun off from the parent company as appropriate. Examples of this are Lucent from ATT; and Orange from Hutchinson - which has successfully continued to bounce in and out of telecoms: Vodafone, KPN and France Telecom. Ventures for developing ATM's, robotics, and personal computers were among a whole series of independent concepts that followed IBM's Lou Gerstner and his team's strategic decision to use entrepreneurship to stimulate growth.

> **Organisations operate more productively
> with fewer resources when entrepreneurial.**

The project must clearly define the resources expected from the design through to realisation or non-realisation of it. Allotting a good budget sends a clear signal that the organisation has a strategy that is committed towards entrepreneurship. Conversely, allotting merely a token budget will result in the organisation not recognising the importance of the project and many will consider that valuable resources are being thrown away on a trivial exercise. When this happens other essential resources in the form of talented 'best assets' will ignore calls to join the project.

Establishing resource commitment is vital for a projects success but, I hasten to add, an organisation intent on becoming more entrepreneurial will, in fact, discover that it can operate more productively with fewer resources.

I believe that the benefits that can be derived from setting up a separate unit to run entrepreneurial initiatives with a specific allocation of resources can easily counter any of the arguments that can be raised against such a policy.

The best route to develop entrepreneurial leaders and instil that elusive sense of 'ownership' is for them to experience running a start-up business unit. Though millions, billions in the case of some corporations, of dollars are quite correctly invested in research and development, products and services are of little value if their benefits are never realised because of a lack of effective entrepreneurial leadership.

6. Concept Value Recognition together with Contribution & Risk Reward

Entrepreneurship involves willingly risking from concept to implementation to maximise value. The motivations therefore that stimulate entrepreneurship are to receive recognition for the value that a concept has been instrumental in delivering and to receive reward that reflects both the risk element involved and the contribution that was essential to bring it to fruition.

The challenge is clearly to be able to measure both the value gained and the contribution invested. The more traditional performance related compensation is neither conducive to entrepreneurship nor an incentive for entrepreneurially-minded employees to stay. The fact is that both value and contribution can be measured and terms mutually agreed when the time is specifically undertaken to do so.

From a shareholders and stakeholders perspective they must accept that high reward levels proportionate to contribution and risk will have to be made. If not they risk losing any such future contribution to a competitor. This is not because of some greed factor. It is more a case that corporations seeking the benefits of instilling ownership, greater creativity, innovative products, good customer relations and market share will have to deliver proportionate return to their entrepreneurial leaders.

In one generation Vodafone went from a small mobile phone operator to head up the elite of UK business as rated by the FT 100. Among many entrepreneurial ventures was the successful $80Bn acquisition of the German operator, Mannesman. Yet resistance in delivering proportionate compensation to the CEO Chris Gent was based on opinions that his compensation was already sufficient. Gent's ardent loyalty to, and exceptional leadership of, Vodafone was never in question – but the shareholders would certainly have paid in greater terms had Gent departed.

When opinions formed by comparisons are used as the basis for compensation, such opinion holders restrict entrepreneurship. Delivering the largest ever cheque of some $50m dollars to Tom Cruise for his participation in the movie *Mission Impossible* as part of his upfront and mutually agreed percentage for his contribution to the movies success and associated products, Columbia stated that he was worth every cent.

When Steve Jobs took only $1 a year for 1998 and 1999 it was on the agreed basis that upon delivering what was expected of him he would receive 20m Apple shares. He delivered and his pay package as valued by Fortune Magazine for 2000 was £381m.

Applying the essential O.I.L.S. of Entrepreneurship

Born in 1889, Haroldson Lafayette Hunt left his parents' small farm in Illinois at 15 years of age. Working as a cowboy and labourer he saved enough to buy a cotton plantation in Arkansas. Floods and agricultural depression caused it to fail. While recouping capital to start anew he considered what would be the next opportunity. Hearing that oil had been discovered in El Dorado, Arkansas, he immediately went there and began trading in oil leases.

During the great depression he looked only for opportunity. He identified a region of East Texas though it was not considered to contain oil. Yet, once again in moving quickly towards the area of opportunity he learned that there had been some wildcat drilling. Recognising the implications of investing in such opportunity he chose to take the significant risk, but in his mind it was a calculated investment, to buy land and leases. To the sizable capital required he displayed real innovation; he reportedly played in a poker game and won.

The area, Daisy Bradford 3, became the largest oil field in the world at that time and is still producing. Within five years H.L. Hunt was a billionaire in today's relative terms and under his leadership Hunt Oil continued to grow through active opportunity seeking and unusual innovative thinking. Being interviewed many years later he remarked along the lines of: 'When you know what you want, you are able to recognise your opportunity. Once you do that, the "how to do it" seems to find you. Sadly most people go through life without ever knowing what they want and the few that do, delay doing something about it until it's too late.'

A generation after his death, Hunt Oil continues to follow the founder's philosophy of drilling for oil in places where others do not think to look. Rich oil fields have been discovered nationally and internationally including the North Sea and the Arabian Peninsula – in areas believed to be devoid of oil. This latter required real innovative service, as it demanded the construction of over 250 miles of pipeline across the mountainous terrain to the Red Sea. Corporations today that seek their Fortune (500 rating) must look to drill for those very same O.I.L.S. that Hunt used to discover his oils. Similarly they must be looked for in areas too often perceived as devoid of them.

But they do exist and comprise the attributes of:

Opportunity. Innovation. Leadership. Service

Drilling for such O.I.L.S. today is essential to evolve toward entrepreneurship. The successful organisation tomorrow will have to ensure that they are in abundance. Hunt heard about opportunity because he was actively looking. Upon hearing about them he actively investigated and got involved in order to understand. The innovations he employed were based on what his experience at the time guided him to do. He was more interested in the why not, rather than the how to. Clearly he had leadership attributes and a service philosophy or Hunt Oil would not have continued as it has.

These four factors are essential for entrepreneurship and form the basis of entrepreneurial organisations. Where opportunity and innovation can be likened to the incoming yin of a business, leadership and service can be paralleled to the outgoing yang. Where one exists in less proportion to another that part of the business will be adversely affected. Innovation, leadership and service are dealt with in greater depth in Parts 2 & 3.

Opportunity-Focused

For now it is important to understand that the very raison d'être for entrepreneurship is derived from opportunity. The common perception of entrepreneurship being risk-focused is very much a myth. The very basis of entrepreneurship requires a willingness to take ownership so risk-taking is viewed very responsibly. Entrepreneurship is more likely to reduce risk by using or hiring a resource rather than just owning it. All business of course involves some element of risk as indeed the very act of living does. As the saying goes: to live and not to risk, is not to be born. But the main point is that entrepreneurship is *opportunity-focused*. Without opportunity to capture there would be no need for entrepreneurs. Conversely, without the entrepreneurship within us opportunity would be neither sought nor seen.

Waiting for the tide to turn

The true meaning of opportunity originates from a time long before modern harbours when a ship had to wait for the full flood tide before it could make it into port. Aware that the cargo in their hold represented the fruit of all their ventures, the whole company aboard ship would be on the look out for the full flood tide that would carry them towards success. They knew that if they missed it they could lose their fortune to another ship competing for the same market. At the moment the tide was spotted the cry *ob porto* would be shouted. Indeed Shakespeare wove the implications of winning or losing opportunity when he wrote in his play Julius Caesar:

> *There is a tide in the affairs of men,*
> *Which, taken at the flood, leads on to fortune;*
> *Omitted, all the voyages of their life*
> *Are bound in shallows and in miseries.*
> *On such a full sea are we now afloat;*
> *And we must take the current when it serves,*
> *Or lose our ventures.*

Entrepreneurship involves seeking and pursuing opportunity. Successful entrepreneurship is capturing the value from opportunity. But how can we know what is a good opportunity? One that is right for us and will create both value and reward? Many established organisations are understandably confused when, despite their expensive market research and development, they witness smaller or new competitors create value from what would be a perfect opportunity for them. The way an business perceives

79

opportunity will of course influence what they expect to see from their market research. But the main influence is that the models they rely on relate to monitoring recognised markets. They do not monitor unrecognised markets. Established markets may earn revenue, but establishing markets create value. And opportunities are about creating value. Points to be aware of in seeking opportunity are highlighted in Table 2.5.

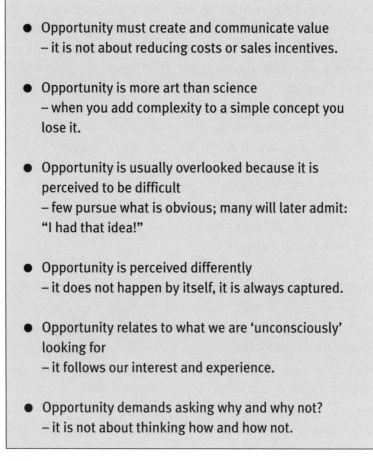

- Opportunity must create and communicate value
  – it is not about reducing costs or sales incentives.

- Opportunity is more art than science
  – when you add complexity to a simple concept you lose it.

- Opportunity is usually overlooked because it is perceived to be difficult
  – few pursue what is obvious; many will later admit: "I had that idea!"

- Opportunity is perceived differently
  – it does not happen by itself, it is always captured.

- Opportunity relates to what we are 'unconsciously' looking for
  – it follows our interest and experience.

- Opportunity demands asking why and why not?
  – it is not about thinking how and how not.

Table 2.5

Opportunity is everywhere and in abundance. Which is why discernment is essential. We have to know what it is we want and why we want it. The fact is we unconsciously gravitate to that which is most dominant in our mind. From an organisational perspective it is important to be aware of both growth trends and growth markets and their differences.

In the early 1980's I became aware of a trend towards changing the use of town centre warehouses to shopping centres. There has always been a market for elderly people to be close to shops. New planning policies reflected this by suggesting that slightly off town centre areas would be viewed favourably for what was referred to, at the time, as 'sheltered housing' – apartment blocks or residential units with a resident warden and low parking requirements. Blending trend with proven market, I recognised the opportunity to create value by acquiring options on sites, gaining planning permission and either selling or developing the sites. Sticking to the regions that I and my various surveyors, architects and agents had well researched, we successfully identified and gained permission for many ideal sites either having first negotiated a purchase or acquired options to purchase. Approaching emerging 'sheltered homes' building specialists in both standard and exclusive ends of the market we developed relationships with companies that later become the market leaders respectively: McCarthy & Stone and English Courtyard Association.

> **Entrepreneurship involves seeking and pursuing opportunity. Successful entrepreneurship captures the value from opportunity.**

In due course the trend's interest dropped as the market became established. At this time I recognised the emerging trend for theme restaurants. There has always been a market for food and dining but the venues with informal atmosphere, friendly service, good food and value for money were few and far between, particularly in the UK. Identifying small buildings of character in places that people really like to go, such as quays and old towns, Piaf's was born.

Based on the famous French singer Edith Piaf our bistros were compared with the highly popular television series and London West End show *'allo 'allo*. This was good because I had purposely mimicked the sitcom. The success of the venture could be measured by the queues of customers trailing right down the street to gain entry. We gave them complementary wine and garlic bread while they waited, even umbrellas if it was raining. Few establishments would consider such entrepreneurial service for building loyalty and long-term relationships. As we sought to expand with other themes it became clear that once again the trend had satisfied the market and we sold them on.

Entrepreneurship is about seeking *new* opportunity, capturing it and creating value out of it. It is not about holding on until being caught out by it. Opportunity and adversity are inextricably linked. The adversity minus sign becomes positive when it crosses with opportunity.

The next trends for me were SkyPark Business Units at Airports and then exclusive HQ's in the country close to facilities and communications. Once again both these trends blended with the proven market that people need places to work. The key is recognising the trends of what people want. Because they are the market and when people lose interest, the market becomes bored, and when that happens the tide of opportunity is about to turn once more. And no amount of organisational board meetings can change the moment. Only entrepreneurship can capture it.

The Student Entrepreneurial Leader

For an individual to evolve from employeeship to entrepreneurship it requires overcoming previous 'conditioning.' A conditioning that fundamentally taught: 'do as you're told,' 'know your place' and 'don't bite off more than you can chew' as essential prerequisites for getting by. But who wants to just get by?

What business will succeed in the future by just getting by? Individuals and organisations must recondition themselves to embracing the concept of taking and giving ownership respectively. In each of our hearts we have a passion to chase. Yet, we become far too concerned about securing our pension. There is infinitely more security, however, in chasing our passion than worrying about our pension.

In the east there is wise aphorism that the best master never loses his passion for learning. For the moment he stops being a student he brings his evolution to a standstill and can no longer lead others. In the west there is an increasing understanding that the best organisations must be places of learning or they will not progress. Both these factors are vital for success because the best way to learn is to teach. Leaders must therefore be students and vice-versa.

Successful organisations tomorrow will comprise students that learn and apply effectively both the principles and practices of entrepreneurial leadership.

Part Two:
Passion v Pension

Chapter 3
The real P.R.I.N.C.I.P.L.E.S of Entrepreneurial Leadership

Chapter 4
The right P.R.A.C.T.I.C.E.S of Entrepreneurial Leadership

Chapter 3
The real P.R.I.N.C.I.P.L.E.S of Entrepreneurial Leadership

ULTIMATELY MASTERING THE PRINCIPLES and practices of entrepreneurial leadership is a process that demands the unified growth of three elements. These three are personal development of the individual, teamwork effectiveness and organisational change. Too often, however, these three elements do not grow in unison. Take, for example, the individual having chosen to engage in personal development. Regrettably, sooner than later, he or she discovers that they see things differently to both the team they work with and the corporation they serve. What happens?

Usually colleagues are very quick to put down the individual's first enthusiastic approach with the comment: 'don't mind them, they've been on a course – but don't worry they'll soon back to normal.' The individual's second, more sincere approach, is to try and initiate changes within their team or organisation. Often after this they feel isolated. A third more determined approach is to get tough. This gives their colleagues an excuse to isolate them further. Depending on their persistence, and their status level, these various approaches work to some degree, but usually only in the short-term.

Then the fourth reflective approach of 'why do I waste my time here' comes to them. From this point the individual will either fall back on the security of previously discarded habits or take the opportunity to leave. This route may be of value to the person, though detrimental to the organisation. Yet they do so not because they really want to but because they have reached a level of dissatisfaction with what they do. Having worked hard to develop their potential they want to continue to grow rather than be held back by small-mindedness and security worries.

They want to be able to serve and be valued for the person they have worked hard to become. It is for the same reason that many relationships fall apart, when one grows and the other party wants to maintain things just the way they are. With relationships unless there is mutual growth and respect they are doomed to either fail or drift along bound only together through habit. Similarly, from the organisational perspective, any change program that does not personally develop its people and continue to do so, through building entrepreneurial thinking and ownership, will inevitably be unsustainable and be viewed as just another fad with the common refrain of: 'here we go again, another change program' voiced between corridors and emails.

Should it be any surprise that organisations do not retain good people? The percentages of people that leave corporations are unnecessarily high. To invest millions of dollars in training for the benefit of your competition may be common practice, but to retain the brilliance that an organisation has been instrumental in developing makes much more sense.

From a team perspective, many successful competitors of established organisations have been set up because whole teams, having developed together, feel held back by either individuals within the organisation or the organisational structure itself.

The whole point of entrepreneurial leadership is that it brings the best out of the individual, the team and the organisation. Entrepreneurial Leadership is: *instilling the confidence to think, behave and act with entrepreneurship in the interests of fully realising the intended purpose of the organisation to the beneficial growth of all stakeholders involved*, where entrepreneurship *involves willingly working together*. The two chapters in this part of the book comprise the following sections intended to help you learn, apply, teach and instil the principles and practices that will develop the attributes of entrepreneurial leadership throughout an organisation.

PURPOSEFUL: the real objectives

To be purposeful means to be determined, to have focus, to be resolute, decisive and persistent. Indeed the virtues that the successful fruition of any objective demands. Undeniably, it is the one human quality that is most sought after in life, yet it is generally found lacking in most people.

Man without purpose has often been likened to a ship in the midst of an ocean that has lost both its rudder and sails. When all is calm the dilemma often goes unnoticed, except perhaps for a distinct lack of firm direction or decisive motion. Should the weather change it will be submerged by external influences. But we can still lose sight of our objectives even with our sails and rudder metaphorically in place. Unless you *purposefully* take action, you will be driven in the wrong direction. As Ella Wheeler Wilcox aptly describes in her poem 'Fate':

> *One ship drives east, and another drives west,*
> *With the self-same winds that blow.*
> *'Tis the set of the sails, and not the gales*
> *Which tell us the way they go.*
>
> *Like the waves of the sea are the ways of fate*
> *As we voyage along thru life.*
> *'Tis the set of the soul which decides its goal*
> *And not the calm or the strife.*

A few years ago I was invited to a traditional tea ceremony in the boardroom of PHP (Peace and Happiness through Prosperity) an Institute founded by Konosuke Matsushita with a mission to promote individual and organisational prosperity through continuous improvement; today one of Japan's most influential businesses. The teacup presented to me was from the early Edo period (1650). After the ceremony I was given a composition, by Matsushita entitled *Velvet Glove, Iron Fist*, which included a story of Ikeda Mitsumasa, a famous Warrior Lord of the early Edo period. The story related that to bring the best out of yourself, your colleagues, your team and your organisation you must be purposeful. To be purposeful you must strike a balance between severity and leniency. Metaphorically speaking your hand must be like an iron fist in a velvet glove.

PRINCIPLES	PRACTICES
PURPOSEFUL:	The real objectives ...the right **P**EOPLE
RESPONSIBLE:	The real accountabilities ...the right **R**OLE
INTEGRITY:	The real values ...the right **A**TTITUDE
NONCONFORMITY:	The real creativities ...the right **C**OMMUNICATION
COURAGEOUS:	The real strengths ...the right **T**EAMWORK
INTUITIVE:	The real decisions ...the right **I**NNOVATION
PATIENCE:	The real relationships ...the right **C**USTOMER
LISTEN:	The real markets ...the right **E**NERGY
ENTHUSIASM:	The real communications ...the right **S**UPPORT
SERVICE:	The real actions

If you are always praising others to get the best out of them they will become complacent and not develop. Conversely, if you are always reprimanding them for not doing their job properly, they will be reluctant to approach you with new ideas. There is a balancing act that has to be performed. Colleagues should know that your support to them would help them be the best they can and produce good results. But they should also be aware that an element of toughness lies under the surface. Unless you have this toughness it is not possible to be purposeful. Unless it is wrapped in tenderness your purposefulness will lose its force.

It is this extraordinary combination of tough and tenderness that distinguishes a real entrepreneurial leader such as Jack Welch. A meeting with Jeff Immelt, before he became his chosen successor to lead GE, illustrates this. After a long day that had still not resolved a difficult issue, Jeff announced that he was tired and wanted to go to bed. Welch cornered him, put his arm around him and said: 'Jeff, I'm your biggest fan, but you just had the worst year in the company. I love you, and I know you can do better. But I'm going to take you out if you can't get it fixed.'

Some four years later when he did pass the crown to Jeff Immelt as his successor, Welch said: 'I'm excited to be leaving, and I'd be feeling horrible if I had any doubts about Jeff.'

Welch believes you have to be hard to be soft. 'Only successful companies are able to be nice to their people and you are not going to be successful if you are not hard', he says. Welch applied his philosophy at GE in what some may argue were brutal terms, for example, all managers have to fire the worst 10% of their staff each year. The fact is that GE has been one of the most consistently successful and entrepreneurial corporations from its foundation by Edison right through to the last phenomenal two decades under Welch's entrepreneurial leadership. Clearly, the organisation's philosophy honed by its various leaders was conducive to developing entrepreneurial leaders. Jeff Immelt was chosen from within the company because as Welch says, 'he was the most purposeful.'

Within two weeks of being handed the crown Immelt's purposefulness was tested to the full. Following the horrific terrorist outrage on the World Trade Centre on the September 11th 2001 that shocked the whole world, GE's continued outlook for prosperity looked bleak. Immelt's purposeful announcement to maintain double-digit growth, however, generated a confidence that rallied the whole stock market to take a more positive stance.

Thriving on uncertainty

To harness the principle of being purposeful is to establish a personal mission, align it to your organisational mission and set goals within the framework of those missions. I believe that it is easier to do this than to not do so. My argument stems from questioning: Why do we tolerate bad leaders? Why do we put up with unfair criticism, obstructive colleagues, lack of support and unclear objectives, broken promises and thoughtlessness? If we do then it follows that we must be guilty of these offences too. For, if we were not, we would not be prepared to put up with them. I also believe that to the degree that we do put up with the bad is proportionate to our lack of purposefulness. It follows that to the degree we demand the best is proportionate to how purposeful we are. To accept anything less is neither to value what we do nor who we are. Yet all too often we accept the bad because we are more certain of it.

We live in an age of uncertainty, yet we continue to seek our security in certainty. Traditional organisational leadership requires a climate of certainty. Entrepreneurial leadership thrives on uncertainty. The main difference is that where the former will seek to establish limits; the latter will look beyond them. In testing for purposefulness the questions to ask are:

1. Have you established a personal mission?
2. Are you committed to your organizational mission?
3. Is there alignment between the two?
4. Do you take daily action to fulfil your missions?
5. Are you able to articulate your missions to others?

6. Are you upset when others break their promises to you?
7. Do you keep your promises to yourself?
8. Are you resolute when doubt questions what you have done?
9. Do you feel secure when the outcome is uncertain?
10. Does the unexpected influence your actions?

11. Do you always receive clarity from leaders for your objectives?
12. Does pursuing your objectives bring out the best in you?
13. Do your objectives bring out the best in others?
14. Do colleagues support you because they want to?
15. Do you set deadlines for yourself and others?

These questions are effective in getting us to reflect and review, because they initially require a simple yes or no. Being able to answer *yes* to every question indicates that you are purposeful. In wanting to answer yes more than having to say *no* indicates that inside you have the aspiration to be purposeful. In having to admit *no* more times than *yes* unfortunately indicates that you are unclear on what the real objectives in your life or business are.

Though they can be answered with a simple yes at first, the root of each question demands soul-searching, personal evaluation and hard-won experience just to be able to answer yes. Questions 1-5, for example, demand immense consideration because the very nature of knowing and then aligning what you personally are with what you professionally do, then internalising it to the point that you can articulate to others to gain their support, is the very essence of successful leadership blended with purposeful action. Answering such questions should not be an attempt to judge one's self, but rather to assist in determining what is required to be one's self. How to develop such alignment has been explained in my previous works *Born to Succeed* and *The Eureka Principle*. My intention here is to identify what is required to be purposeful.

Purposeful Objectives in Action

Hiroshi Okuda, chairman of Toyota, and his team are an example of an organisation that displays the purposeful principle. To them their clear objective is serving the world with high quality good value cars that require minimal service. Toyota's economic value creation has no equal in the industry. The corporation has maintained its market share over the past 20 years, despite attempts from competitors to erode it, because of its ability to increase production and meet the needs of its customers.

One of the key factors for their success is always cultivating the basics. For example, continuously refining the conveyor belt system pioneered by Henry Ford in order to eliminate waste at every point of the assembly line; develop just in time supply chains; and keep costs lower than the prices that customers are willing to pay.

To expand their global presence and maintain their research and development, meet dividends and annual expenditure they maintain a $20Bn reserve. Analysts have speculated that with such a war chest companies such as BMW may be targeted. But Toyota have no intention of increasing their global reach through acquisition as Ford did with taking Volvo, Land Rover, Mazda and GM did in buying Saab and shares in Fiat Auto, Suzuki and Isuzu. Add on deals and larger takeovers are not the real objectives. They concentrate instead on investing in localised production and design. Even more than this though, as Mr Okuda says, 'it is our purposeful objective to eradicate defects and ensure that every Toyota is built to a high standard – this will solve all other problems.'

A purposeful leader is only as capable as the company that surrounds him. Welch chose Immelt from a company that had Welch and Immelt qualities in abundance. Mr Okuda heads a company that shares objectives. Alexander the Great led from the front but he surrounded himself with a team of elite bodyguards that had been trained by him. He had hired the best and then sought to bring out the best in them. When Alexander died the team that had developed with him were able to keep many successor kingdoms going for centuries.

Remember that to be purposeful means to be determined, to have focus, to be resolute, decisive and persistent and to be tough. An entrepreneurial leader must be thoughtful enough to bring out the best in people even it means being tough.

> **A purposeful leader is only as capable as the company that surrounds him.**

RESPONSIBLE: the real accountabilities

Leaving school at 15 Gerald Ronson had in abundance the one qualification essential to succeed in life: the desire to chase a *passion*. We all have it but too many of us have submerged, rather than chased it. In its place we gain a different qualification, which, all too often, turns out to be unsatisfying in abundance; the desire to chase a *pension*.

It is of course being responsible to arrange a pension, but it is also being responsible to ourselves to chase our passion. Indeed, it is our greatest responsibility; if we cannot be responsible to our selves, how can we be responsible to others?

We may not be always responsible for the responsibilities of others, but we are always responsible for whether we ultimately succeed or fail. In business terms chasing our passion will take care of our success while securing our pension into the bargain. It can only be due to our conditioning that we believe chasing our passion is being irresponsible. For chasing it involves being accountable, though with a solution-focused paradigm (mind-set or frame of reference), rather than a blame-focused paradigm. Too often the business world is focused on finding out who is to blame for problems. This is why there is reluctance to take ownership or be accountable as such action (operating a blame-focused paradigm) may risk the pension.

In chasing his passion Gerald Ronson built the UK's largest and most profitable private company, Heron. Revolutionising petrol retailing in the 1970's Ronson pioneered the concepts of self-service sites, canopies and forecourt shops. If it wasn't for him we wouldn't be able to get late-night snacks, nor fill up our cars at two in the morning. He had the vision to realise that people want convenience when they go shopping.

With Heron becoming the UK's largest independent retailer with commendation for management training and commissions to advise on petroleum marketing internationally, Ronson went on to amass a further fortune with his entrepreneurial property group, Heron International, the UK's leading private building company. In 1990 he went to prison.

Gerald Ronson was one of four, including the chairman of Guinness, Ernest Saunders, found guilty of colluding in an unlawful share support operation to guarantee success of the $4bn Guinness takeover of Distillers four years earlier.

Despite arguing that he had been denied a fair trial Ronson was jailed and fined a record $7m. The DTI (Dept of Trade & Industry) had been determined to make an example of what they believed to be conspiracy. Permission to appeal to the House of Lords was refused. Indeed, one of the 'conspirators' Jack Lyons, was stripped of his knighthood, awarded earlier for good work to charity and business. It was not until ten years later that the European Court of Human Right in Strasbourg ruled that Ronson had been denied a fair trial.

A model prisoner and even termed 'the gov'nr' by fellow inmates, Ronson was released after six months. At the same time the full slump of the early 1990's was causing Heron Group to stagger towards insolvency under debts of $2bn. The DTI and press veterans waited daily for news that receivers had marched into Heron's London Headquarters.

It never came. Bankers and creditors ultimately had more confidence in the passion chasing man who left school at 15 than in the pension laden hugely expensive insolvency practitioners. Their faith was bolstered because of Ronson's openness about the group's problems and his realistic assessment of the surgery required. He considered his real accountability to the Heron Corporation and the people who had made it be the success it was. His plan involved having to give up almost all of his family's entire stake in the group, and disposing of almost all of the self-service stations he had painstaking developed.

Heron survived and in due course developed billion-dollar leisure and shopping developments throughout Europe. Having anticipated the demand for both self-service stations and shops on garage forecourts Ronson then went against the trend for Internet shopping believing that entertainment led twenty four hour shopping centres are what customers want. Once again he has been proved right. His prediction that: as lower value standardised shopping moves towards internet and TV shopping, retail complexes will be forced to add value or die, is coming true. There has been a progressive shift in retailing to a more lifestyle and entertainment focused activity.

Recently Gerald Ronson won the Property Personality of the Year award. The award was voted for by a telephone poll of the property industry and the man at the helm of the internationally renowned Heron Group emerged as a clear winner. The reasons were because property people respect a survivor, entrepreneurial developments, a person who retains the loyalty of both colleagues and friends and the responsibility to do what has to be done.

Today Heron is a major international property force renown for having built a dedicated team of people with experience, intuition and expertise in developing and managing property to maximise it value. Though Heron had scores of self-service gas stations Ronson took it upon himself to visit every one of them regularly. His management, motivation and service approach has won Industry Training Awards – co-incidentally a division of the 'DTI.'

Retaining the confidence and loyalty of your people, your friends, your creditors and your peer group irrespective of how much your world changes is the true measure of success. To create a culture around you where everyone believes 'if it's to be, it's up to me' does require a passion that makes even providence come to your aid. Conversely Guinness Chairman, Ernest Saunders, was caught on the 'who's to blame' side of the double-edged sword of accountability, when a cowardly board ditched him as soon as the going got tough.

Organisations that operate under a pointing the blame leadership will not be able to develop the entrepreneurial environment that will grow real accountability. People want to be responsible but they do not want to be used as scapegoats. That old testament policy related in Leviticus when all the (religious) leaders hold a ceremony to place all the blame for their ills on a tied up goat and then allow it to escape, is a classic example of avoiding accountability.

Admitting you are wrong takes courage, resolving to put everything right by being responsible takes experience. Experience gained through being allowed to make mistakes in the knowledge that there is loyal support behind you. Julius Caesar's passion and responsible actions built an empire. Yet when times changed as they always do in the cycles of life, he gave his life in the name of accountability. His deepest regret being the disloyalty he felt at the hand of his closest ally, Brutus. Metaphorically killing off colleagues by blaming is not the way of entrepreneurial leadership.

The *'what kind of company would my company be, if everyone in it was just like me'* questions to ask our selves are:

1. Do you seek to blame others?

        Always   Sometimes   Never

2. Do you cover your tracks if things go wrong?

        Always   Sometimes   Never

3. Do you laugh about others' mistakes?

        Always   Sometimes   Never

4. How often do you deny responsibility?

        Always   Sometimes   Never

5. Are you critical of others' irresponsibility?

        Always   Sometimes   Never

6. Do you agree to be accountable?

        Always   Sometimes   Never

7. Do you propose ownership of a problem?

        Always   Sometimes   Never

8. Do you volunteer: 'my fault?'

        Always   Sometimes   Never

9. Do you give loyalty to your colleagues?

        Always   Sometimes   Never

10. Are you passionate in what you do?

        Always   Sometimes   Never

11. Do you delegate your responsibilities?

        Always   Sometimes   Never

12. Do you prioritise your responsibilities?

        Always   Sometimes   Never

13. Do you follow through your responsibilities?

        Always   Sometimes   Never

14. Do you explain othersí responsibilities?

        Always   Sometimes   Never

15. Do you teach responsibility by example?

        Always   Sometimes   Never

Instilling real accountabilities in our selves requires regular evaluation. The habit of knowing how responsible we are with regard to our thinking and actions is a valuable habit to build. Instilling real accountability in others requires regular praising and appraising. Such a habit will develop a deeper loyalty and greater understanding as to the responsibilities we expect of others.

Most traditional appraisals are too far apart and based on a 'how you can do better' paradigm rather than a 'how well you have done' paradigm. Appraising should include exactly what the words' meaning intends: to both evaluate and praise. In this way appraisals can be used to bring the best out of everyone.

The real accountability of entrepreneurial leaders is to develop themselves and others to the point that questions 1-5 can be answered with a 'never;' questions 6-10 can be answered with an 'always' and questions 11-15 can be answered with a 'sometimes.'

> **Admitting you are wrong takes courage, resolving to put everything right by being responsible takes experience.**

Actual formal appraisals should be done at least every three months yet informal praising and confidence building should be done whenever the opportunity arises. Creating value out of opportunity is, after all, what entrepreneurship is about. If we cannot take the opportunity to develop others then they will not have the same loyalty or motivation to be responsible to pursue opportunity for their organisation.

INTEGRITY: The real values

There is no single quality that defines leaders, whether entrepreneurial minded or not. But an indispensable one is doing the right thing based on a sense of honour and respect toward others. Knowing the right thing to do and actually doing it is having integrity. The Greek philosopher Socrates believed that to really know what is right made it impossible not to act in accordance with it. When he had been sentenced to death by the government for what were considered as highly controversial views, his friends urged him to escape with a plan they had devised. Socrates firmly rejected the suggestion with the reply: 'All of my life I have preached that people must obey the law of the land. If the law is wrong then we should revise it by discussion, and although I am a victim of injustice, I cannot suddenly go against my beliefs just because my life is forfeit. Man's first priority is not just to live, but to lead a good and just life.' In giving up his life rather than live without his integrity he set a great example about practicing what you preach.

As a leader, if you preach something and practice the opposite to save yourself, you will never convince anyone. Nixon was forced from the Presidential office because he was judged as a man without integrity. Integrity is the quality that makes people trust you. And trust in turn is the basis of strong relationships. Without trust there can be no relationship, and certainly not a working one. Human nature being what it is, you may not be able to live up to such a principle 100 percent of the time. Nevertheless the entrepreneurial leader who lacks it will be unable to build the loyal climate so important for sharing opportunity and innovative ideas. Indeed, I believe that the entrepreneurial organisation's greatest ally is the loyal support, whether morally or financially, gained from a reputation of integrity.

Sharing some more of my own experience will illustrate this. In June of 1989 the local manager of a national company of 'valuers' took me for no-expense spared lunch with a view to winning my business. From the start I had made it clear that I was content with my existing group of property surveyors and valuers with whom I had a good working relationship. The local manager informed me that he was of course already aware of this, but sincerely believed that, having done some research on my property portfolio, and knowing my policy of borrowing dollar for dollar, that is 50% of the full value, he would be able to provide valuations that would allow me to buy more property. With the current downturn in property I would be able to pick up some excellent deals. His comments understandably interested me and I asked what level of valuation he was talking about. It turned out to be some 30% above the assessment that my existing valuers had currently provided for me. Though impressed that the manager was talking on behalf of one of the UK's leading valuers I declined to change from my existing one.

Just three months later this same manager called me on the telephone to say that my bank had instructed his company nationally. Apparently, this was in response to major UK banks receiving directives to cut back and review property lending, due to recession concerns. It had fallen on him to carry out reviews on local portfolios including mine. I reminded him that, as he had just recently done research and even recommended a figure, this should not pose too much difficulty for him. He agreed but made the comment that his instructions were from the bank and as such could not be divulged from an ethical point of view. I expected nothing less and hung up.

Ten days later I received a letter from my bank informing me that upon reviewing their lending it appeared that they were overexposed and I would have to reduce debt without delay. I learned that the valuations had been 40% below the original assessments and over 65% below the assessment made by the same valuer who had tried to win my business some three months earlier. Such figures meant that all of my own equity had disappeared and borrowing liability had increased to 100% of value. From banking terms this was unacceptable. You can imagine how quickly I went around to the valuer. But it was of little use. He merely kept repeating how professional ethics prevented him from discussing clients' valuations.

The difficulty with values is that people hide behind them but rarely live by them. Integrity can be likened to high budget marketing campaigns that promise everything, and then don't deliver. A feeling of being cheated lingers like a bad taste in the mouth. What's important is that so long as you declare with integrity you must act and follow through with integrity. It that way, no matter what the challenge, you will always win through. With various meetings between my existing valuer, bank and my own company a resolution was eventually agreed. But the point was made that it was only because of my track record based on loyalty and integrity that I was allowed further support to resolve the situation.

That being said the 1990's recession was a time when regrettably track record was rarely taken into account. Funding situations very quickly began to use the excuse of 'just following orders' when forcing major long established companies out of business. Indeed, my own bank manager a veteran of such events chose early retirement rather than have to foreclose on so many of his long-term clients. His replacement must have been chosen for his inability, or refusal, to see opportunity within adversity. His criteria were simple: if over exposed – foreclose.

Discovering Real Values

While I was facilitating the development of a mission and core values statement for a newly formed satellite of a major telecom organisation, there was a proposal from the group I was working with not to bother with any of the traditional values. 'Yes it's important to know our objective,' they argued, 'but to support the achievement of that objective with meaningless platitudes, comparable to what every other organisation in the industry seems to have, is a waste of time when we should be looking to do things that make us stand out from the crowd.' I agreed that where core values do become meaningless platitudes they are more an impediment to growth than having no core value statement at all. But I went on to argue that in any core value statement it was not, in fact, the words that contained the meaning – it was the manner in which the organisation's people acted that was important. It was the way in which they interpreted the meaning behind developing the statement; not merely the existence of the words themselves.

Therefore, if the group was unable to see how the values that were embodied in the statement could help them, then they would not be able to articulate such values to either their people or their customers in a way that would result in gaining support and loyalty. In such circumstances, the statement would indeed be a meaningless platitude and it would be better to do without it. But the importance of having and living the core value statement could never be understated. The nature of business, particularly entrepreneurial business, is that if you cannot rely on support and loyalty from others then any 'start-up' will soon become a 'non-starter'. And as indicated, that loyalty and support comes from delivering the reality of the words in the core value statement.

The feeling within the group was that as the parent company already espoused all the traditional values there was no need to duplicate the values and they should instead concentrate on quality and innovative marketing to increase sales. Due to bad experiences of developing core values with the parent company one of the key figures in the group was firmly against importing the same difficulties into the satellite operation. Such an association of ideas, where a present or current event is adversely influenced because of an earlier failure is not uncommon. I therefore decided to take each one of the proposed values in turn and test it for what meaning it had for the group.

Taking quality first I asked: if in a few years one of your products becomes such a necessity that the only criteria is how fast consumers can have it, will you delay delivery of it due to quality control demands and risk losing your sales to emerging competitors? The answer was no. Our product might be the best but if we were going to be left with inventory while consumers are content to buy inferior products we would have to be less concerned about quality. It was agreed that the nature of quality, which more often than not was based on the customer's perception in the case of something like transistors, should be placed in a company strategy and not as a core value.

With regard to innovative marketing I asked first: if the demand for products was so successful that you could never match supply would you continue to increase demand; and second: if, by the time it came to market, a particular product was either not wanted or obsolete, would you look to marketing techniques that inevitably would have to comprise of empty promises? As the answers to both of these questions were no, it was similarly decided to regard innovative marketing as a current strategy. Strategies must change to fit circumstance, core values cannot irrespective of circumstance. The satellite unit chose to adopt, yet adapt, the core values of its parent, which included integrity, in the form of 'respect for how we go to market.'

The most important part of the process that they went through was that they were able to discover what their real values were in such a way that they would be willing to articulate them to both their internal and external customers: their people and their consumers respectively. It is not possible to just create something that sounds right in marketing terms. For it to be real you have to be able to feel it emotionally as well as intellectually. Real values cannot be manufactured. They have to be discovered deep down in you. Entrepreneurial leaders display their core values because it is clear to everyone that they hold them passionately at their gut level. If they do not then they are not real values based on honesty and respect. Questions to ask yourself honestly in order to assist in discovering your real values are in Table 3.1

> **Strategies must change to fit circumstance,**
> **core values cannot irrespective of circumstance.**

NONCONFORMITY: the real creativities

Entrepreneurial leaders are not conformists, except in their adherence to their core values. No one achieves the lasting success of being themself by being a conformist. Yet in business, many people stick rigidly to patterns they believe some nebulous majority as decreed are prerequisites for approval and success. In this way business falls prey to a fundamental myth – that the majority is automatically and invariably right. But the majority is not omniscient simply because it is the majority and hardly guarantees the validity of opinion. People who have ignored opinion have spawned more creative success. Such a person is Jim Clark.

Though most of us have benefited from his innovations few people have ever heard of the entrepreneurial leader that has been instrumental in building three separate billion-dollar corporations from start-up. The special effects at the movies we enjoy are because of him. We can universally access the Internet because of him. We can obtain medical assistance online because of him.

1. Do you know what is really important to you about your work?	Y	N
2. Do you know what is really important to you about your company?	Y	N
3. Do you know what excites you the most about what you do?	Y	N
4. Do you know what annoys you the most about your company?	Y	N
5. Do you know what is it that makes you proud when asked what you do?	Y	N
6. What is really important about your work?		
7. What is your own prime value?		
8. What is the prime value that distinguishes your company?		
9. What is the prime value you recognise in others?		
10. If you had to vote against your prime value, but in doing so you were promised certain promotion allowing you to achieve your goals, how would you vote?	Y	N

Table 3.1

After being expelled from School he went on to get a PhD in computer science. Fired at 38 years old for insubordination by the New York Institute of Technology, Clark went on to found Silicon Graphics. Aided by Stanford graduates that were interested in his creative technology and the chip he designed that processed three-dimensional graphics in real time, Silicon Graphics became the world's leader in highest performance computer technology. Their complex visualisation solutions and products dramatically influenced the movie, aviation, automotive, life sciences, defence, media and manufacturing industries.

Ousted from the board of the company he founded, Clark then started Netscape. He didn't invent the Internet. That was indirectly the Pentagon looking for a way to send classified information. Nor did he invent the World Wide Web. That was the researcher, Tim Berners-Lee. Nor did he invent the Web Browser with a graphical interface. That was a pair of Illinois University students Marc Andressen and Eric Bina. What Clark did with his first product, Netscape Navigator was make the Net universally accessible. In teaming up with Andressen he brought the web to mainstream and Netscape Communications became the catalyst for one of history's greatest economic booms. Clark then went on to found Healtheon.

One of his challenges at Netscape was competition from Microsoft, which indeed led to a landmark case for large organisations. Learning from such experience he agreed to a merger with WebMD, part of the Microsoft Corporation, ensuring Healtheon's leadership in the online healthcare market. As Clark commented at the time of the merger: 'Business is a very dynamic thing. You've got to do the right thing for everybody. I've been most successful sharing with others. So in other words, don't try to keep it all. A hallmark of this era is making the wealth distribution within an enterprise more democratic. Everyone gets to share in it.'

Clark won't invest in companies that don't share enough stock with employees. Any other system he considers to be unfair, because companies aren't built by individuals, they are built by teams of people. Clark believes that:

'They are like a tribe of people with a common set of goals and to the extent that you can have all the people honestly contribute you make them a part of the process. You make them a shareholder. You make them win when the company wins. This may be going against traditional opinion but such nonconformity is essential for the entrepreneurial spirit.'

In the early days Clark may have been pure entrepreneur, but after he was ousted from Silicon Graphics by what he termed as the 'money people' he recognised that he must blend his skills with good leadership and management attributes to his future businesses. To create an entrepreneurial corporation you must surround yourself with good people. He believes that pioneering groundbreaking ideas like MyCFO (a financial information Web site) and Shutterfly (an Internet photo developer company) his more recent ventures, demand a foundation of innovative entrepreneurial professionals that must be talented, pull their own weight and be their own person. Clark advocates: 'that more than ordinary leadership is required, because you want them to be both leaders and creative at the same time.' It comes from a combination of being persuasive; believing in what you're doing; having integrity and knowing how to judge good people, because you can't afford to have anything but good people early on in a company.

The conformist is not born, they are made. Indeed, the incessant pressure that bombards individuals, in order that they can be permitted to climb the ladder of acceptance towards success, comes from all sides, only differing slightly from generation to generation. For example: 'yes, you can rebel, but the time will come when you will have to make your own way – and that way must be the established way.' In wanting to achieve success and wealth young individuals already brainwashed on how they should ensure their security, will adopt the clothes and manner of what is considered to be the successful stereotype. The truth is we go where we hope to go, and further, when we give up trying to look and act like everyone else.

To often we dismiss our own brilliant ideas and thoughts, simply because they are our own. Those who follow their hearts are always initially misunderstood, even maligned, before being applauded and leaving their mark. They are guided by what is right for them and not what is right for society.

The achievers of the innovative and information hungry business world will more than ever continue to be nonconformist. But to be unconventional simply for the sake of nonconformity is not what it is about. Those who dress and eat differently to others because it is the fashion to do so, or simply to be noticed, are only conforming to the rebelliousness accepted by society. The true nonconformist dresses and behaves, either unconventionally or conventionally, because that is how they feel comfortable. That is the way they are. It is not to get noticed, be different or labeled rebellious. It is just being themselves. Being a nonconformist is having the courage to say 'no' to something because it conflicts with your own path. Even if the majority would give their eyeteeth to say 'yes' for the same thing.

Executives who crosses swords with their superiors may sometimes risk their jobs in the process. But a business that will fire someone merely because they have the courage of their convictions is not the place a really good executive would want to work. Any business where people are afraid to say what they believe, make mistakes or be radically innovative in the interests of the company will only be successful in developing seasoned conformists. A place where, simply because a status quo has been established, it must rigidly be preserved. Answer the questions in Table 3.2 to test your nonconformity.

The degree that we are externally influenced is in direct proportion to our conformism. To worry and fret about things that are superficial and trivial, even down to wearing what is considered the right clothes, driving the right car and living in the appropriate dwelling, is to cocoon ourselves in the culture of what others consider is best for us. To unquestionably copy those who follow the artificial path, that we have been persuaded to think is the only path, is to abandon our individuality. When we do that we relinquish our ability to innovate and in its place imitate. I believe that our nonconformity or conformity is measured by our creativity or lack of creativity respectively. The more absurd our ideas, the more nonconformist we are. In the words of the creative nonconformist Einstein: If, at first, an idea is not absurd then there is no hope for it.

1.You are at a conference and a joke is made which you do not find either funny or clever. Everyone laughs the 'corporate laugh' because 'someone important' told it.
Do you join in the laughter?

Always   Sometimes   Never

2. At a meeting a colleague has an idea that everyone discards as a non-starter. You realise that you are the only other person that thinks it's worth further discussion.
Do you suggest further discussion?

Always   Sometimes   Never

3. You are involved in a project that you really believe in. A strict budget means that your project will be scrapped in favor of another that you do not believe will work. Your colleagues agree with you, but feel they should join the other project.
What do you do?

4. King George IV of England developed a new style in footwear in the 1820's. The entrepreneurial thinking concerning his boots was copied and is commonplace today, but at the time was very unusual.
What was it? (Answer in Index under K)

5.You are invited to an exclusive event at short notice. You have already committed yourself to be elsewhere.
Do you alter your plans?

Always   Sometimes   Never

Table 3.2

> **Any organisation where people are afraid
> to say what they believe, make mistakes
> or be radically innovative in the interests
> of the company will only be successful
> in developing seasoned conformists.**

COURAGEOUS: the real strengths

When you have the courage of your convictions and the courage to be your own person and follow the path that you believe is best, your real strengths naturally develop. In an earlier work I argued against the commonly used SWOT analysis and I introduced as an alternative the SOM analysis. The SWOT analysis is applied regularly in organisational business. Here Strengths, Weaknesses, Opportunities and Threats are reviewed and considered, yet the category of weakness takes precedent over what is considered strong. Every report will highlight more of the former than the latter in the sincere, albeit misguided belief, that what is wrong must be brought to attention.

Because of this tendency the SWOT analysis could more appropriately be referred to as: Seek Weaknesses Only Test. More time is invariably spent with the salesperson over the sales he or she didn't close, than those that were successfully closed. More time will be spent with the secretary or clerk over errors made rather than discussing any ideas they may have. More time is spent with the receptionist over explaining recording procedures than on client communication either by telephone or in person. Tests are designed to find out what people are not good at, rather than to discover what they are.

The most effective way to develop strengths and opportunities is to ignore anything else. Applying the Strengths, Opportunities and Merits analysis, SOM, will focus the attention on what is, in the end, the only element of any importance. When you identify what your strengths are and focus solely on them, your weaknesses do not count. In excelling in what you are brilliant at, your weaknesses become unimportant. Remember, athletes ensure that they only train at what they are good at. In doing so they are remembered for what they can do, rather than what they can't do.

When a company starts out it concentrates on its strengths, yet no sooner does it become established than its concern is to correct its weaknesses. Similarly parents are delighted about what their young offspring can do; yet as the child gets older the parents can become concerned about what their child cannot do. Starting school, both parents and teachers focus on discussing what a child is good at. Later both focus on the lowest marks in a report.

Trying to succeed in our weakest area results in low self-esteem, a poor self-image and limited self-ideal. These are the elements that make up that influential command centre in our life, the self-concept. Is it any wonder that self-acceptance goes right out the window, when we have been trained to focus our attention on what we must do to correct ourselves, rather than what we can do to excel?

Learning to recognise our strengths and developing the courage to use them effectively is essential. Imagine, for example, a plain white wall as a metaphor for a well-run, successful business. Now imagine that there is a small black mark somewhere on it. Where does your focus of attention go? It travels to the blemish. The established thinking of 'let's fix what's wrong', has become so obsessive that we can spot the flaw in seconds simply because that is what we are looking out for. How many times are we missing strengths by habitually searching for the bad?

No one likes having fault found with what they do; yet everyone has the inclination to do just that with others. The inclination exists because of the belief that, in finding fault, we are being supportive. Although there is nothing fundamentally wrong in a SWOT analysis, it is the application of it that is self-defeating. Applying the SOM analysis strengthens your thinking. Over the next seven days apply it to whatever you are involved with, as well as yourself. Only consider strengths and opportunities. Do not even entertain or consider any ideas relating to weaknesses, or threats, of any nature. Those corporations that have tried this exercise over the past few years have fully embraced the concept because of the dramatic success they have experienced with it.

The main point of the exercise is to place the emphasis on how you can improve what you can do, rather than improve what you can't do. Rather than seek to discover why one team does not communicate or perform, seek to discover why another team does and plan to do more of it. Rather than seek to learn why people complain, seek to discover why they do not and do more of it.

When you have become conscious of where the emphasis of your thinking is applied, you can then consider weaknesses and threats, as you will place them in their proper perspective; to be aware of them in order that they do not get in your way. SOMing up rather than SWOTing down allows you to find out what you are good at and do more of it; and to find out what you are not good at so that you can stop doing it.

One particular client, The Database Group of the UK was turned around from a $500,000 loss to a $500,000 profit in just over a year. I am not suggesting that this was the sole factor involved but as the Chairman Les O'Reilly said:

'It was the fundamental change in our thinking that bought about our success. Where before we were concerned about losing contracts to competition our focus moved toward how we could use our strengths to ensure we would be the ideal choice. When we concentrated on what we could do we saw alternative ways and acted on ideas that we had either previously overlooked or discarded.'

The company went from strength to strength eventually merging with the International Primedia Group. Often it takes something to go wrong to bring the best of our strengths out of us. With Les O'Reilly's Database Group it was having his back to the wall. With Stelios Haji-Ioannou of the Easy Group it was a disaster that changed his thinking as to the kind of businessman he wanted to be. On April 11 1991 a Troodus oil tanker anchored off Genoa exploded during routine maintenance killing five crew members and swamping the Italian coast with Iranian Crude. Referring to it as a traumatic experience that was to shape his life, Stelios was determined to build a group that focused on making a difference and that utilised his strengths to the full. The average age in his Stelmar Shipping Company is 7 years compared with the industry average of 15 years, but his philosophy is if you think safety is expensive try having an accident. Questions to ask in identifying and applying strengths are listed in the box below.

1. What most absorbs you in your work?
2. What movie roles do you associate with?
3. What was your favourite subject at school?
4. What do you day dream about?
5. What sport do you most like to do?

6. Do you delegate what you are not good at?
7. During a difficult time for you what did you decide?
8. What is a recurring resolution for you?
9. Do you know what others expect of you?
10. Do you know what your 3 greatest strengths are?

11. Do you feel confident when you apply your strengths?
12. Do you find you get better when you use them?
13. Do you feel frustrated when you are not able to use them?
14. Do you get good rewards because of your strengths?
15. Do you believe that you are applying them to the full?

Being courageous is so closely linked with entrepreneurial leadership that it is not possible for the one to exist without the other. In all of our lives there have been occasions when we have been tested to the full yet it is because of such times that we become reacquainted with our real strengths. As the emperor philosopher Seneca said: It is not because life is difficult that we do not dare, it is because we do not dare that life is difficult. Unless we dare to discover, use and apply our strengths we will forever experience a sense of mediocrity that causes us frustration and emptiness. Moreover we will be unable to assist in discovering, using and applying the strengths of others. It takes courage to aspire to be who we really are and develop our strengths to the full, but we serve both society and our organisations better through our aspirations than through our frustrations.

> **No one likes having fault found with what they do; though the inclination is to do just that with others. Learning to recognise our strengths and developing the courage to use them effectively is essential.**

INTUITIVE: the real decisions

A real decision is something of major importance. Not what you are going to eat, where you are going on holiday or even what car you are going to buy. Real decisions are those that affect your future and success and those of others. Few would argue that one of the most important skills in business is to get on with others. I believe that it is of equal importance to make *right* decisions. 'Of course it is!' I can imagine you are saying to yourself. Life would be as perfect as it could get if this were the case, but it is hard enough to make decisions, let alone always make the right ones. I contend that each of us can learn how to become intuitive to the point that the really important decisions we have to take, whether large or small can, with practice, increasingly be the right ones.

Any decision of course to be taken should really be made after all available information has been digested. This is good common sense but there is not always the opportunity to collate all available information, in which case we tend to then rely on our reasoning. Indeed rationalising about what choice we should take is the basis of our decision taking. Some people expound the virtue of solely using our intuition to make decisions. But the real art of using intuition is guiding us towards making good judgment, not replace it.

Harnessing our intuition for decision-making is vital for the entrepreneurial leader. In *Born to Succeed* I explained the proven steps to activate our super-conscious or 'genius' through which our intuitive faculty comes, a faculty that can be deliberately cultivated and consciously trained. Later in *The Eureka Principle* I discussed how to use our intuitive power to increase our natural creativity and communication abilities. This book assumes that the reader has practiced and understood these steps. Even if not understand that intuition is a capacity that each of us is born with, like the capacity for breathing and eating.

When we breathe properly the lymphatic functions essential to our health improve over one thousand percent. When we eat properly our mental and emotional well-being improves significantly. When we recognize our intuitive guidance our decisions are always right. It is amazing that many of us neither breathe nor eat properly. One might, therefore, suspect that few leaders have confidence in their intuitive based decision-making. It is a misconception that intuition is a power we acquire. We were born with it for the reason of survival. Only the most intuitive of our ancestors would survive in the harshness of their early surroundings. Our competitive surroundings today are of no less importance, as they can be just as harsh.

A further myth is that women are more intuitive than men. This misconception is based on the belief that the former use it more consistently. Traditionally men refer to hunches and gut feelings rather than admit they have what is more associated with feminine realms. Fortunately this is changing. The fact is that regardless of gender, a partner will invariably come up with an intuitive course of action that proves the right one. Often this is because, uninfluenced by the weight of information available, they are able to heed their intuition with more clarity. The skill, however, is to combine our intuitive capacity together with all the knowledge we have on a matter and make our decision accordingly. The real decisions must involve intellect, emotion and intuition. In others words does it add up right, does it feel right and does it *sound* right? When applied to making real decisions these factors must be used in unison.

Surprisingly effective

Though her early decision was to go into law, because she believed it was expected, and with her Stanford degree it added up right, Carly Fiorina, quit law school after a few months because it neither felt nor sounded right for her. Never even imagining a business career, having grown up in an academic community, Carly, however, joined a real estate investment brokerage, Marcus & Millichap, as a receptionist. The offices were opposite the Headquarters of Hewlett

Packard. She learned the basics of commerce for a year and then went to Italy to teach English. She then decided that business school was the thing for her. 'Choosing business school was surprising, yet absolutely right for me,' she said. 'Don't let your options paralyse you. Make a decision because it both sounds and feels right and then choose what happens next.'

Joining the business world in 1980, she spent nearly twenty years at AT&T and Lucent Technologies expanding the international business and later planning and implementing Lucent's spin off. When the call came through unexpectedly for her to lead Hewlett Packard she had no illusions about the magnitude of the challenge in leading a company that had a great past, but was searching for its future. Arriving early for what was the interview of her life with the HP board of directors, she drove into the parking lot of the Marcus & Millichap offices that were still there. Understandably she thought about how life was coming full circle in some unexpected yet seemingly right ways. As she sat in her car she felt humbled by a great sense of responsibility for a great legacy. 'I weighed up the challenge, how I was such an unexpected choice and the scrutiny and criticism that such a position would attract.' She didn't feel afraid in deciding to take the position she was being offered because it both sounded and seemed right and later recalled that the day she walked into HP for the first time as new CEO it felt both utterly surprising and surprisingly familiar.

Under Carly Fiorina's leadership, HP has returned to its roots of innovation and inventiveness and is focused on delivering the best total customer service. Working towards this objective she described HP's merger with the computer organisation, Compaq, to create a new global giant as a 'decisive move that positions us to win by offering even more value to our customers and partners.' As Chairman and CEO of the combined organisations the new company has operations in over 160 countries and ranks No. 1 worldwide in its industry. Fiorina understands the importance of re-developing both the entrepreneurial and engineering skills that were instrumental in HP's heritage and indeed encapsulated in its slogan: 'Invent.'

To help keep both the edge in engineering and innovation while making HP people more adaptable and responsive, compensation relates to improvements in customer-approval ratings. To develop a greater awareness for entrepreneurial leadership at all levels of the organisation, the concept of 360-degree feedback was introduced. But she also ardently believes that both heart and action must be totally aligned for in doing so we are able to be true to ourselves and open to receive the intuitiveness so essential in making the real decisions.

When asked to deliver a lecture to graduates at Stanford University, 25 years after her own graduation, she proposed that they ask the following questions:

- Am I acting out a role, or am I living the truth?
- Am I still making choices, or have I simply stopped choosing?
- Am I in a place that engages the mind, and captures the heart?
- Am I stuck in the past, or am I defining my future?

Questioning decisions

It is important in life to know what questions we should be asking. The life of one person is different to another because of the questions they ask of themselves. For, without question, it is our decisions that shape our future. Asking the opinion of another when making a decision and then blaming them when things do not turn out right is a common enough path to the future. But it is clearly a path in the wrong direction as far as using our intuitive powers are concerned.

It is actually an unnatural condition to not know which way to turn when we are faced with real decisions. Not trusting our own intuition comes from not really believing in our abilities, or that we do not deserve something. We can only confidently trust in our intuition by simply being aware when something does *sound* right to us and having the courage to follow it through. Confidence is built through risking that our intuition will be right. Risking builds confidence and in turn confidence allows us to risk. When we become accustomed to confidently risking that our intuition will be right for us we overcome our fear. In doing so we overcome the world.

There are four questions to apply whenever faced with a decision or a situation that requires a decision. The questions are based on the four psychological processes that we engage when we evaluate situations. The first is: How does this add up? It involves what you know based on your knowledge, your memories and what you are able to find out. To be able to answer this you need to have investigated, collated and digested all the information that you are able to lay your hands on. If you are unable to do this or cannot be bothered to take the time to do so, then the decision cannot be defined as a real decision.

The second question is: What do I think about this? This involves your judgment and interpretation. As your perceptions influence both your judgment and interpretation of what you have to decide it is important to be aware of whether the decision conflicts with what you believe to be right for you.

The third is: How does this decision feel to me? You will either feel comfortable about it or not. Most physical ailments come from pain associated with having to make a decision or putting off an important decision. Billionaire philanthropist and investor, George Soros, used the onset of pain as a signal that something was wrong with his portfolio. Intellectually aware that this was hardly a logical way to build a portfolio he nonetheless consciously relied on such indications as intuitive messages informing him that his logic was incorrect. Whenever he felt uncomfortable about something he would review until he 'felt' right.

The final question is: How does this sound? This involves what we can intuit about the decision to be made. When we have gathered together all the information and we feel comfortable, it is important to then become aware as to how it sounds to us. Very often we will come across something that sounds too good to be true, even though all the available data makes for a good case. Sometimes we may come across something that sounds right to us, even though the information we have is scant and what we have does not add up. When something sounds right it is as though we have come across it before and are simply rediscovering a path that we just know is right for us. It is this sense that we must become aware of, as it is the most important part of real decision-making.

In relying on others for answers, as a child, we begin the process of distrusting our intuition. Re-learning to trust out intuition requires acknowledging that for every question that faces us, the answer lies within. We will always know the answer but only by learning to have faith in that answer, irrespective of the risk we might perceive in it, will we hear it with clarity. In Table 3.3 there are five 'real' deciding questions that may or may not be currently applicable to you. In answering them apply the four-question procedure of:

1. What do I know about this?
    (How do the facts add up?)
2. What do I think about this?
    (What is my interpretation?)
3. What do I feel about this?
    (Are my emotions are affected?)
4. What do I intuit about this?
    (Does it sound right?)

Remember that the answers that come to you will seldom seem logical at first. Often it is not until after the event that we can see the clarity and wisdom of our decision. What is important is to be honest with yourself so that you are able to trust your judgment.

1. **Should I apply for the position that will soon be available?**
   - What do I know about this?
   - What do I think about this?
   - What do I feel about this?
   - What do I intuit about this?
2. **Should I continue with the project I am working on?**
   - What do I know about this?
   - What do I think about this?
   - What do I feel about this?
   - What do I intuit about this?
3. **Is this acquisition/merger/disposal/ the right way to go?**
   - What do I know about this?
   - What do I think about this?
   - What do I feel about this?
   - What do I intuit about this?
4. **Will this relationship/partnership be for the best?**
   - What do I know about this?
   - What do I think about this?
   - What do I feel about this?
   - What do I intuit about this?
5. **Am I really fulfilling my current role effectively?**
   - What do I know about this?
   - What do I think about this?
   - What do I feel about this?
   - What do I intuit about this?

Table 3.3

When we are busy being somebody for everybody, it is nigh impossible to be either our self or trust our self. When we are unable to trust our intuition we instead build barriers of preconceived opinions, formed of intellectual pride and prejudice.

> **Re-learning to trust our intuition requires acknowledging that for every question that faces us, the answer lies within.**

With such barriers the tendency is to view others as masters and sources, instead of the teachers and agencies that they really are. Developing a confident trust in our intuitive ability to make real decisions through clarity of questioning increases the flow and frequency of the right answers. Being aware of and receptive to this flow of answers, which often come in the form of further questions, is a fundamental requirement for aspiring entrepreneurial leaders to practice and perfect.

PATIENCE: the real relationships

Man is unique in placing time constraints on the results that he wants in life, particularly where relationships are concerned. It is of course far easier to be patient for something when the outcome of it is certain, because in our certainty, there is less room for anxiety. There is a direct correlation between patience and certainty as there is between impatience and doubt. The more impatient you are for something to go the way you want, the more you begin to question whether it will.

Whenever, for example, you question an intuitive idea you once believed right, your questioning causes increasing doubt until you think the idea absurd and either ignore or distort it to fit into rational constraints. Although the idea was right, your rationale, influenced by your impatience to get where you're going, perceives it as either wrong or too slow a route to what you want.

Being patient requires greater confidence in what we are working towards. And we build greater confidence when we learn to patiently work on the process of what we are doing rather than impatiently waiting for the result of our efforts. The immediate obstacle is accepting that we can only control the process of what we do. We can have no control over the actual result. This concept is alien enough to our conditioned thinking because it requires being-process focused rather than result-focused but when you patiently work on the process, outcomes become more certain.

When we think only of the result our emotional attachment to it unwittingly interferes with the essential process. Yet in applying this concept, one begins to recognise that it is a *natural* way of thinking, particularly in relationships. For patience with another reflects the measure of the patience we have with ourselves. This is the basis of the paradox that patience produces quicker results, than impatience. Such paradoxical thinking demands a high level of awareness though.

Consider those difficulties that have caused you to re-evaluate your life in order to overcome them. Such reflection reveals that having patience would have made things easier. Because when you are impatient to get out of, or for that matter to get into, something you are more liable to compromise yourself.

Often when we decide we want something, we want it sooner rather than later, and when we don't get it, we feel that life is unfair. We convince ourselves that it is because others, and even forces beyond us, do not want us to have what we want. In taking things personally, we convince ourselves that the acquisition of our desires is at the mercy of the inquisition by others.

Yet being impatient is simply an obstacle to overcome. To build patience, it is important to acknowledge obstacles as opportunities to strengthen you, not indications of failure. This mirrors the wisdom of the Chinese writing symbols that contain the meanings of both crisis and opportunity. For in such flexibility lies the power to cultivate the hidden pearl of opportunity from the grit of adversity.

One Step at a Time

Patience is the fundamental key in both building and sustaining relationships. Impatience is the nemesis of customer relationships. Though initially assailed by top consultants for its go-slow approach to Internet grocery selling, the enduring Tesco is became the world's largest online grocer. The competitor that it was advised to emulate, the eager Webvan, one of the most richly funded start-ups in history, failed. The story illustrates the importance of recreating entrepreneurship within established organisations and of ensuring that entrepreneurs cultivate management attributes.

Jack Cohen, an immigrant, founded Tesco in the 1920's selling his groceries from carts. He patiently built up the business to be one of the leading supermarkets in the UK.

As with many 'established' organisations the strengths of service and quality can sometimes become complacently overlooked. Tesco was no different in experiencing this during its growth and for many decades was left eating the dust of the market leader, Sainsbury. After an internal executive power struggle in the 1990's, won by marketing head Sir Terry Leahy, Tesco obsessively focused on customer relationships and soon became outright market leader. In 1996 when Internet shopping began to seem a fantastic idea, Tesco's approach was very reserved. Though a giant with available funds they chose to take one step at a time and tested just one market from a chosen store for the first year. No extra facilities such as warehouses or personal were put in place. Shelf pickers would simply fulfil orders and arrange delivery.

Conversely, Webvan started out running. Though none of the board members had grocery industry experience, and there were no existing suppliers or customers, they aimed to enter 20 US markets within 12 months and spent $1.2bn building automated warehouses. Dependant on web sales alone, Webvan wooed customers with free delivery, losing up to $30 on every order it fulfilled and continued to build facilities though none of its warehouses were breaking even.

Emulating Jack Cohen, CEO of Tesco.com John Browett, chose a distinctly low-tech approach. Instead of building state of the art distribution centres he built up to handling almost four million annual orders with a 1950's delivery-boy type system. It is important to be patient when dealing with customers and profits: 'You can't make a run for revenues and then work out the cost structure later,' advocates Browett. Advised to have warehouse structure and to not charge for delivery, Browett ignored both. Using existing facilities it duplicated the process that had worked at the first store soon reaching a third of its 690 outlets delivering to over 90% of the population in the UK. The fixed delivery fee of $7.25 actually encouraged customers to place larger orders. Indeed Tesco received about $27m a year in fees in 2000.

Browett admits that there were doubting times because while the hype was at its peak, they were keeping the costs very marginal; $58m dollars against Webvan's $1.2bn. Yet the high cost Internet marketing model that turns to disaster clearly confirms the wisdom that the patient tortoise will win over the impatient hare every time.

---

1. **Are you patient when others do not understand you?**
   Always   Sometimes   Never
2. **Are you patient when the deadline cannot be met?**
   Always   Sometimes   Never
3. **Do you give others your undivided attention?**
   Always   Sometimes   Never
4. **Are you results or process focused in your actions?**
   Always   Sometimes   Never
5. **Does a lack of financial resources make you impatient?**
   Always   Sometimes   Never

Table 3.4

In answering the questions in Table 3.4 you can quickly learn your patience quota. If you are inclined towards the metaphorical tortoise you will answer with always/ sometimes. This is because you are confident in what you are about and have a certainty that everything happens at the right time and in the right place. If you are more inclined towards the metaphorical hare you will answer with sometimes/never. This is because you believe that unless you get things sooner than later you will miss out on the opportunity.

Seeking out and creating opportunity is one thing. To capitalise and maximise opportunity requires the involvement of others and usually strong, loyal relationships; such are built patiently, one step at a time. The entrepreneurial leader needs to be patient with developing both people and customers.

Both people and customers dislike being rushed and indeed feel less valued when they are so. When I first went on line from my home to 'test' the Tesco system my property did not register with them because of its location. Upon calling the 'any difficulties' line this was immediately resolved and deliveries to suit me were commenced. It was not possible to do so immediately however and I was thanked in advance for my patience. Truly we do not mind being patient when that which is promised is shortly delivered. Too often corporations indulge customers' patience or a colleague's patience only to abuse it by non-delivery or lack of support respectively.

> **We build greater confidence when we learn to work patiently on the process of what we are doing rather than impatiently waiting for the result of our efforts.**

LISTEN: the real markets

Marketing is a term that was originally intended to illustrate how the success of a business lies entirely outside of itself. Marketing teaches that if we listen to external economies, society and our customers we can use the information to determine internal strategy. Amazingly, marketing is seldom used for this. Rather than ask 'who is our customer' it has become just a tool to support selling by asking 'how can we sell more of what we want.' Having now moved from a culture of selling products to serving customers, it is now more important than ever that we listen to our markets and determine what is wanted.

Listening is vital in business, particularly in three main areas, yet seldom is time dedicated to any of them. The first area relates to anyone who has major responsibilities to undertake. They should have someone who knows how to listen. Without such a valuable 'lieutenant' they will find in hard to succeed in their important roles. Having the opportunity to air doubts and frustrations and generally get things off your chest permits you to keep on track despite the obstacles ahead and ensures that you put your abilities to best advantage.

The second area is that anyone involved in a responsible position should always be willing to listen to colleagues' ideas and concerns. People who know that their boss will listen every time they have something to say and will respect their ideas are more inclined to think creatively. It instils confidence and stimulates them to come up with new ideas and observations that will contribute to improvement in work.

Conversely, people who are conscious of the fact that their boss is not willing to listen, will increasingly become bored and apathetic and their confidence level drops. The more their ideas are ignored the less they mention them and exercise their creative imagination. Both these elements relate to different levels of mentoring, discussed in further detail in Chapter 5, because such successful listening is part and parcel of building an entrepreneurial culture.

The third area relates to listening in such a way as to become aware of the real markets are to focus on even if it goes contrary to the analysts. The founder of *USA Today*, Al Neuharth, related an experience that illustrates the importance of going to where your 'audience goes,' in order to listen and learn. As an assistant to Lee Hill of the *Detroit Free Press* he was invited to lunch by Jack Knight, owner of the *Knight Rider* chain of which the *Detroit Free Press* was part. They went to the up-market Detroit Club where they had a cocktail then left. The surprised Neuharth enquired about lunch and Knight took him to down town to a basement lunch counter.

The multi-millionaire and Pulitzer Prize winner, Knight, ordered hot dogs and coke for them and said:

'Lee Hill will give you memberships in the best clubs and get you to meet the mayor and other dignitaries and after a while you will think that you are writing for them. But *remember* the people that buy our papers eat *here* every day. Don't ever become a captive of your own comfort or you will forget to listen to your real market. Keep your feet on the street and don't eat at the Detroit Club everyday.'

Neuharth directly applied what he had learned from that experience to the operations of *USA Today* as a popular national tabloid. Knowing what your real market is and listening to what it wants may sound like common sense but it is certainly not common practice. Usually 'considered opinion' is sought first and with such analysis resulting in strategy paralysis.

Howard Schultz, chairman of Starbucks, hired analysts to determine the market prospects for the US coffee Giant in Japan and the verdict was severe. Though they conceded that the stores might be slightly successful in trendy Tokyo, the non-smoking rule, unheard of in smoke-filled Japanese coffee houses, would turn off customers. Furthermore no self-respecting Japanese would risk losing face to walk the street with a paper cup. Listening to real market opinion, rather than relying on considered opinion, Starbucks tests proved so successful that within a few years there were over 300 stores. Indeed, if you walk down a busy street in Tokyo a regular sight are Starbucks Latte-toting customers.

In deciding to go public, though established and proven, analysts later advised against launching an IPO because the adverse market conditions had been the worst in decades. The ¥17.9bn listing, however, proved to be one of the most successful in 2001 opening at 25% higher than the anticipated set price.

Starbucks did not listen to how they could sell more, they listened to what customers wanted: good quality delicious selections of coffee, conveniently and in surroundings conducive for conversation – better than at home.

The entrepreneurial leader must be aware of the market they are involved in and actively listen to it. Major competitors are respectful of those leaders that have the courage to follow through their active listening even though the consultants will argue that the market is not ready. While industry leaders and bankers fretted about the prospects for 3G (third generation mobile communications service) Keiji Tachikawa, the president of NTT DoCoMo launched it ahead of all others.

Mr Tachikawa's decision was based on having listened to customers. With the company's mobile data service, *i-mode* having 28m subscribers it was clear that the market would want faster data services because faster access to data is more convenient.

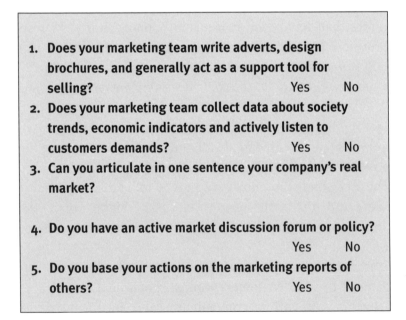

1. **Does your marketing team write adverts, design brochures, and generally act as a support tool for selling?**   Yes   No
2. **Does your marketing team collect data about society trends, economic indicators and actively listen to customers demands?**   Yes   No
3. **Can you articulate in one sentence your company's real market?**

4. **Do you have an active market discussion forum or policy?**   Yes   No
5. **Do you base your actions on the marketing reports of others?**   Yes   No

When *i-mode* was first launched sceptics condemned the idea yet it became the most successful data service in the world and the source of the corporations prosperity. Sir Chris Gent of Vodaphone likened his Japanese rival, Tachikawa, to a brave pioneer charging into a barrage of arrows as he ventures into unknown territory. Though he conceded: 'I am grateful to DoCoMo for being the first.' Tachikawa policy, however, is that an idea should be bold, but the implementation should be steady and based on listening to what is more convenient for them. How about your company?

Entrepreneurial Leaders understand that long-term relationships and prosperity grow through empathy; genuine and active listening. As communication is more about how we feel about what we say than what we actually say this leads us to the penultimate principle.

> **Knowing what your real market is and listening to what it wants, may sound like common sense but it is certainly not common practice.**

ENTHUSIASM: the real communications

Man is born with an optimistic or positive outlook, but the artificial nature of pessimism or negative outlook is allowed to come to the fore. Pessimism comes from disappointment, from a bad impression formed from some hindrance of something past. Perhaps pessimism may show conscientiousness and experience, but what good is it to think only of what difficulties may lay ahead of us? The psychological effect of optimism is such that it helps towards success.

For the optimistic individual it does not matter if things do not come out just right, they will take their chance. For life is an opportunity and as such offers promise for seizing, not withdrawing from. There are many people, however, who prolong a difficult situation by nurturing it with pessimistic thoughts. They unwittingly do so until the condition becomes so real that absence of it seems unnatural. They believe that the state that they experience is normal for them, that such misery is their share in life. An optimist will naturally help another who is drowning in fear or disappointment. A pessimist, conversely, upon meeting such a person will sink them even further into their despair.

Pessimists are just not conducive to communicating with others, however, many people seem to prefer them to people who are overly enthusiastic. Having the tendency to burst the bubble of another because they are being too enthusiastic is almost a form of abuse. Saying something that was once unkindly said to us has the same effect on another as it did on us. The enthusiasm for example, that a new employee feels when first commencing work, should not be dampened down. Yet everyday it is done in countless offices in the name of teaching reality.

Optimism and enthusiasm go hand in hand. One feeds the other. It is not possible, for example, to be enthusiastically pessimistic. Enthusiasm will differ from person to person, but we all recognise when another has it. He or she is passionate about what they do, and their conviction is infectious. We are magically drawn towards the person who exudes natural enthusiasm. We must ask ourselves on a regular basis, how enthusiastic we feel about what we do for it is the basis of how we communicate to others.

Compared to Billy Graham because of his evangelical preaching, the CEO of Cisco Systems, John Chambers, enthusiastically communicates his vision and strategy and people follow him. When I first heard him present I was sold. Numerous awards speak for themselves. In leadership recognition Chambers has been awarded the titles of CEO of the year (*Worth*); Best Boss in America (*20/20*), Best Industry Leader, (*US Internet Council*) and Mr Internet (*Business Week*) to name a few from leading credible periodicals. More importantly Cisco has been designated the US's most dynamic company (*Forbes*); the #3 best place to work and the #3 most admired company in America (*Fortune*); the #1 company to work for in the UK (*The Sunday Times*), to name a few. In five years Chambers grew his organisation under $2bn in annual revenues to $20bn and won the additional award for the fastest company in the US to reach a market capitalization of $500bn.

It was the enthusiasm of Cisco people that placed the company at #1 in the UK. Cisco applies entrepreneurial leadership by trusting its people with highly flexible work patterns and a hands-off management style. 100% of staff reported that they are always willing to go the extra mile to get the job done. Indeed, the majority of new recruits come from employee referrals because they are so enthusiastic about their company.

Cisco's vision and strategy have been communicated and duplicated at every level of the organisation. Communicating real messages to both people and customers is one of the biggest challenges of business but is essential for common focus. Chambers' ambition for Cisco Systems is to grow the Net into the backbone of all communication, changing the way people work, play, live and learn. The culture he values at Cisco is one that prizes time with customers and contributes to their success. He has proved that such a prize is achievable by instilling the passion to do so throughout the company.

From an external perspective, it is the little things, for me, that reflect the nature of a culture. In particular I am always very sensitive to treatment delivered by receptionists as they mirror, to the customer, what a company culture is really like. The Cisco receptionists are so enthusiastic about work that they arrive earlier than required in order to make fresh coffee to greet visitors. Enthusiasm, like pessimism, in an organisation is highly contagious and is duplicated and communicated like wildfire. Indeed bad news travels even faster. It is therefore vital that the people that sit behind the desk are treated in the same way as those customers that stand in front of the desk.

To achieve effectively demands taking the action to serve your people as well as you serve your customers. It also demands recruiting and having people that your customers will like. This, in turn, demands that both new recruits and existing people must love what they do. When they don't they impede the success of an organisation. Because when people do a job for the sake of just earning a 'pension' they will lack the enthusiasm for following a vision with 'passion.'

Passion and pessimism spread like wildfire Communicate and duplicate the right one

It is impossible for CEO Steve Ballmer of Microsoft to hide his devotion when talking to his people. He is known to frequently preface his presentations with a loud outburst of how much he loves the company. Many no doubt watching out of context may of course find his enthusiasm disconcerting but the fact is that the loyalty of his people is clear to see.

In spending time with the Managing Director of Microsoft UK, (now vice-president of Microsoft Eurpope, Middle East & Africa) Neil Holloway, the high level of enthusiasm and loyalty was clearly evident for me to register. Neil loves what he does while recognising the immense responsibility his role carries of serving both his people and customers. 'Any responsible role is carried out more effectively with enthusiasm than without,' he told me. 'Your message may not always be understood at first, but the way you say it will be.' People recognise insincerity. When you really believe in what you are doing your enthusiasm will naturally endorse it.

It is not possible to force people to develop enthusiasm as it comes from within. But when people feel part of something that excites them they 'naturally' become enthusiastic. It is essential to do what you love and if you unsure of what this is then at least learn to love what you do. If what you currently do does not excite you then make a decision to find out why and if necessary adapt your role, or get out and do something that does enthuse you.

The only question to ask, therefore, is: are you serving yourself to the best of your ability? This is so important because we must learn to serve ourselves first. If not how can we learn to serve others effectively? This does not mean putting ourself first, it means putting ourself in order first. It does no good to complain about the street if our own house is not in good order.

SERVICE: the real actions

Everyone knows the importance of customer service. Everyone thinks that they know what good service entails. Yet it is the customer's perceptions that really count. Understanding your customer's perception of you, your product, your service and your business is the key to building long-term relationships and successful sales growth.

We may think that our customer service is fantastic and always 'exceeds expectations.' Yet unless we are able to put ourselves in the shoes of our customers we will not be able to maximise on the value that we are seeking to create from the opportunity of having customers. Receiving feedback from our customers is just as important as receiving feedback about ourself. It helps to evaluate the real actions required.

Entrepreneurship is about having empathy and understanding with those people that will do business with you. Your customers' perception determines value. The key to keeping customers is to ask honest questions about how you can improve your service. Consistent performance is what customers most want from a service company. More specifically this means:

- Doing what you say you are going to do
- Doing it when you say you are going to do it.
- Doing it right the first time
- Getting it done on time.
- Putting yourself in your customer's shoes.
- Taking reliable care of your customers.

That is what will keep them coming back. People may love buying, but dislike being sold to. So forget selling to them and instead treat your customers like lifetime partners. Imagine, for example, that every week they visited you and at the end of each visit they purchased something from you, how would you treat them? Thoughtfully, or thoughtlessly? Using your own company as an example, try to 'perceive' as a 'customer' and answer the questions in Table 3.5 on a scale of 1 to 5 (5 is high). Excluding 13, clearly if you scored a high 5 in each box then your company has a high level of empathy with customers.

Vital to offering entrepreneurial service, is continuous improvement of the individual through personal development. Success in customer service is founded on personal commitment to improvement, alignment to a meaningful mission, enthusiasm, innovation and a passion to bring the very best to their customer. Follow through service is greatly appreciated because it is rarely performed and unexpected.

1. How well do we deliver what we promise? ☐
2. How often do we do things right the first time? ☐
3. How often do we do things right on time? ☐
4. How quickly do we respond to your requests
   for service? ☐
5. How accessible are we when you need to contact us? ☐
6. How helpful and polite are we? ☐
7. How well do we speak your language? ☐
8. How well do we listen to you? ☐
9. How hard do we work at keeping you a satisfied
   customer? ☐
10. How much confidence do you have in our
    products/services?
11. How well do we understand and meet your
    special requests? ☐
12. How would you rate the appearance of our facilities,
    products, communication and people? ☐
13. How would you rate the quality of our
    competitor's service? ☐
14. How willing would you be to buy from us again? ☐
15. How willing would you be to recommend us? ☐
16. Are we doing anything that annoys you? (Answer Yes or No)

(Answer the following with whatever you perceive)................
17. What are we not doing that annoys you.............................
18. What do you like best about what we do? ....
19. How can we better serve you? ....
20. What parts of our service are most important to you?
    ....

Table 3.9

So it is vital to deliver what you promise, say what you mean and mean what you say. Concentrating on how you can help your customers more is a much better principle than the practice of thinking how you can make as many sales as possible.

To deliver profitable service to the customer, it is important to show them that you value what they want more than you value what you do. Customers don't like being let down when they have been promised something will happen. They resent having to wait for a particular service and then be told that such a service is worth waiting for. They feel duped when exciting advertisements offer fantastic service and they are unable to either get through on the phone, or when they finally do, the person on the other end is too busy, indifferent, disinterested, not aware of the offer, just started or even rude.

Cash flow is not the life's blood of a business; customers are, for without them there is no cash flow, there is nothing. When a business fails it is because of lack of custom. If you don't make what people want then no amount of cash flow will help. Often people will make something and then try and market it, blaming marketing and poor sales for not performing. After all, they will say, we know the product is good.

The product may be the best invention since sliced bread, but if every customer around you prefers rice, what good will it do your business? What is required is a full understanding of what customers want to experience, to develop empathy for them. Many service-oriented businesses operate under a false illusion that customers need business. That's getting it backward. Business needs customers for without them there is no revenue, let alone profit. Profit itself should be regarded as the applause for providing good acts of service. So, by providing excellent service we will enjoy the reward of greater applause from our audience.

There are only *two* reasons that *any* customer buys anything: *good feelings* and *right solutions*. People don't want to be sold a house, for example. They want to feel comfort and contentment. They don't want to be sold clothes. They want to feel good about their appearance. They don't want to be sold a computer. They want to feel the benefits that technology can offer. People don't want to be sold *toys*. They want to buy *happy moments* for their children. People like buying. And they buy people not things. That's what develops customer loyalty. Genuinely making them feel good for buying from you and by serving them with the solutions that they want.

Great service requires continuous questioning of existing routines and creating something that brings meaningful value. Routine service is something that customers soon take for granted and therefore don't value. Consequently, whatever you do in a routine way will cause customers to perceive that what you are doing is merely your duty to perform and their right to benefit from.

The only source of competitive advantage that a business has is its people and the service they provide. Therefore all front-line people must be trained to ask themselves: *'how would my action look on the front page of tomorrow*

1. Do not treat customers as just another transaction to be processed
2. Question routines that may be taken for granted
3. Know the importance of putting emotional value in what you do
4. Treat your customers like a friend
5. Focus on turning one-time buyers into lifetime customers
6. Remember that it is the little things that make a difference
7. Never show your customer that they may be wrong
8. Reward the right behaviour to get the right result
9. Be service oriented as that is how your customer perceives you anyway
10. Know that thoughtful service costs less than thoughtless service
11. Do not let 1% of difficult customers influence how you treat your other 99%
12. Regularly ask your customers what they think of your service
13. Set an example through your own customer focused performance
14. Use praise, recognition and reward to motivate your ambassadors
15. Know that rewarding the customer is everyone's responsibility

Table 3.10

morning's newspapers?' What interests a customer is: did you deliver what you promised you would because it was what you said that prompted them to buy from you? Keeping your word is worth more than all the sincere apologies and make-it-up-to-you gifts in the world. Because good customer service that builds loyalty is just far too important to be passed to some customer relations department, everybody must be a customer-service ambassador for their company because that is how the customer perceives it anyway.

Getting everyone, not just customer-contact ambassadors but *everyone*, to ask themselves *'What results do I produce and do they benefit the customer?'* will galvanise everyone to think about the basics of their job in terms of the customer. Through individual or team meetings everyone should be encouraged and guided into setting goals. These goals must be simple and to the point. Each person should only have a couple of goals to focus on at any one time and they should be concisely written for clarity of purpose and commitment. Above all, they must be measurable. Putting your customers first with entrepreneurial service will be your best competitive advantage so it is important to ensure that the following actions in table 3.6 are instilled throughout the organisation.

Service in Action

When an entrepreneurial service starting with just $10,000 investment can expand to over 1,000 customer outlets and generate over $1.5bn in revenue in just 10 years clearly it has hit on the right customer ethos. When Charles Dunstone founded Carphone Warehouse in the UK he did so on the basis not of selling mobile phones but on offering simple, impartial advice. Employee commission was unaffected by which phone or service the customers chose to buy empowering sales consultants to offer the most objective advice.

It was while working with NEC, the Japanese telecommunications giant, that Dunstone identified that small businesses were being poorly served by the mobile communications industry. Teaching and implementing the above points that have been made, Dunstone's entrepreneurial leadership had won his company *Best Customer Service* and *Retail Employer of the Year* awards for consecutive years.

Recognising the vital importance of developing entrepreneurial service toward customers throughout the company, Dunstone's strategy was one of incentive and reward. At flotation of the company everyone with at least one year of service received an award of 300 shares plus 100 shares for every additional year. Even part-timers received an allocation.

To ensure that service philosophy is duplicated prospective recruits must engage upon a two-week induction. A position is only forthcoming should they be successful in passing the exams at the end of the program. Remuneration is well above the average supplemented by performance-based bonuses and benefits include private health insurance, subsidised gym membership, and celebrating success. In 2001 Charles Dunstone became Entrepreneur of the Year awarded by the Foundation for Entrepreneurial Management.

The best way to test a service is by using it of course. I visited many of the Carphone Warehouse stores and was surprised, but certainly refreshingly pleased, that they did in fact deliver what they promised. I say surprised because service in the UK is usually non-existent. Unfortunately, too many businesses are failing to deliver what they promise despite genuine initiatives to boost customer service.

In every successful entrepreneurial business I have either founded, or been involved with, the basic criterion has always been the same. Think service, act service and follow through service equals reward. Yes the product or idea must create added value; but so must the service for success to be sustained. Entrepreneurial leadership involves creating value through service as much as through opportunity.

> **Success in entrepreneurial service is founded on personal commitment to improvement, alignment to a meaningful mission, enthusiasm, innovation and a passion to bring the very best to their customer.**

Chapter 4
The right P.R.A.C.T.I.C.E.S of Entrepreneurial Leadership

THE LESS WE DO SOMETHING, the more we dislike having to make the effort to do it. Even if what we have to do is enjoyable. I know that although I enjoy writing, each time I take a prolonged break from it, it is harder to get started again. It is easier to engage in the distractions that would have otherwise been devoted to writing time. Yet, when ardently involved in a project that requires regular attention, I dislike having to engage in any of the former distractions even though they are enjoyable or important.

Principles work well when they are regularly practiced and indeed overcome bad habits by replacing them with alternative good ones. Practicing my purposeful principle of writing as a real objective, for example, overcomes the bad habit of procrastination by replacing it with the good habit of following things through.

A long-time goal of mine was to own a Harley Davidson. Having experienced a fairly serious motorcycle accident, almost thirty years earlier you can imagine that the goal was not on my priority list. Rather than forget it completely, however, I altered it to only owning one if I lived somewhere warm and dry like the Cote d'Azur. Such rationalisation perhaps prevented me from feeling bad about not achieving a goal. Years later when I considered moving to Europe's Silicon Valley at Sophia Antipolis near Cannes I reflected on my old goal. The rationalisation then, from everybody else, was that I must be experiencing the male menopause! To drive a 1450 cc bike was crazy and there must be another way to capture my youth – didn't I know that my 'age-group' was high risk in such areas! Fortunately, my family supported me because they knew that I would not be stupid enough to get on a bike, and just go. The principle of responsibility means we must be accountable to ourselves first. If I was choosing to fulfil such a goal, I must therefore learn the principles and practice, practice, practice.

When you know what you want you gravitate towards its fulfilment. Prior to moving, I discovered on the Internet that there was a specific Harley Davidson Academy not far from where I lived. Contacting them I explained that it was years since I had ridden a bike. The service and attention was excellent and my teacher, a veteran motorcycle police trainer of 20 years, instilled me with confidence. The one-to-one intensive course commenced with me being taken through all the principles. Then, having understood what was involved, the practice of the principles followed.

Starting on a small bike in a training park I was able to master the principles and rose to the ranks of the Heritage Classic Springer, the exact 1450cc model that for a few weeks had been on my screen saver to assist my visualisation of my goal. At the end of the course my instructor reminded me to never stop practicing. The day I collected my Harley, which was the same model I had practiced on, I was very nervous.

As you get older you become more aware of your vulnerability and it didn't help that near the Italian border where I collected the bike, everyone considers themselves as a practicing Michael Schumacher but without his knowledge of driving principles.

Taking the bike out everyday, to practice, my confidence began to build. At hazardous points in the road my concentration allowed me to even hear the instructors voice in my ear advising, confirming or praising my actions. Often, we will drive to work or home and because we have either been absorbed in our thoughts, the radio, or a more commonly today, a phone call, we arrive at our destination almost unaware of our journey. It is almost as though we have driven on autopilot. The majority of accidents can be traced back to a lack of concentration, or awareness, and often we learn greater awareness because of an accident. I am absolutely certain that if I had practiced sufficiently the principles that I had learned later, my accident all those years ago would have been avoided.

Whenever something is important to us we should be more aware, but it's seldom that we are. Too often we are so involved in the hustle and bustle of business to practice the principles which we know make good sense and lead to success. Promising that someday we will take the time out is not good enough. The world of entrepreneurship may be likened to driving something that we are not quite used to, in surroundings that suddenly appear more hazardous than we initially thought. The habit is to retreat to the comfort of being cocooned in something that we believe to be more secure, where we can relax our concentration, and get somewhere without too much concern as to how we did it. Such a habit must be replaced with acknowledging those principles that will ensure we can achieve our goals and practicing resolutely until we do.

The right PEOPLE

'People make the difference' has been the slogan of many conferences that I have attended. But then it's pretty obvious isn't it? Nothing may be as powerful as an idea whose time has come. But without its implementation by people, the idea is worthless. The common refrain of all successful entrepreneurs is: 'if only I could find someone like me.' Corporate leaders go to great pains to find the right people to succeed them. Politicians like to surround themselves with the right people. They all want to duplicate themselves, because finding the right people is nigh impossible. Yet it can be done, but the practice of first finding them, then developing them, and then retaining them, because they want to, takes practical yet unconventional methods.

The very nature of his explorations demanded that Sir Ernest Shackleton recruited only the right people. The fact that he and all 27 of his men survived being stranded 1200 miles from civilisation on the frozen iced wastes of Antarctic for two years, from 1914 to 1916, and then made an 800 mile trip to rescue themselves from the breaking ice in little more than a rowing boat, arriving in good health and spirits confirms that his recruitment methods were successful. His criterion put their character and disposition before their science and seamanship. They also had to share his vision and enthusiasm for the voyage to be embarked upon and not simply be interested in the status of being an explorer; they must be compatible with others and loyal to others; they must be optimistic and have a sense of humour; and they must be hard workers and really want the job.

Character and disposition are not discovered in career resumes or in constricting application forms. Questions on competency and experience will not ascertain whether someone shares your vision. Checking out references will not ensure loyalty, compatibility or optimism. Traditional interviews will not give guidance as to the desire for the position or how hard a person will work. The only science in selecting people should be chemistry. This is true of any relationship but particularly of entrepreneurship because everyone is 'willingly working, risking, creating, implementing, driving and following through together.' You have to like the people you are going to work with. People may be better for getting to know, but not always. Entrepreneurial leaders should recruit people that have a chemistry that matches their own.

Because being objective may result in finding the wrong person, you have to be subjective. We will always intuitively be sensitive to another; as to their capabilities and character but often such sensitivity remains undetected in the formality of selection processes. In recruiting a crew, Shackleton would first ensure that he found the right person to help him recruit. In taking the time to explain exactly the qualities that were demanded his lieutenant would then be able to identify and select from the hundreds of applications those that he knew Shackleton would want to interview.

Therefore, Shackleton knew that the competence and experience he required was already present. This was good because the questions he would ask did not relate to such things. He would be looking for signs of enthusiasm and team member ability. 'Can you sing?' he would ask, 'Keeping spirits up is a vital survival factor'.

> **People may seem better for knowing, but not always. Entrepreneurial leaders should recruit people that have a chemistry that matches their own.**

Importantly, he sought genuine desire in his recruits. For example, in sending telegrams to the three selected candidates for a final interview the following day, he received one reply back requesting a more convenient day and one proposing that there be some guarantee of a job before making another long trip. Not hearing from the third he was about to leave his office when, a dishevelled individual burst in clutching his telegram. Though he had been on a walking trip some 250 miles away the telegram had been forwarded to his lodgings. He had left immediately for London taking what trains he could in order to be there. Shackleton hired him on the spot because of the clear commitment.

Identifying and Fostering

It helps to accept that in identifying the right people there are three categories they fall into. People either work against you, for you or with you. For the sake of clarity: if people are working against you, then they should not be working for you. There is only one option and that is getting rid of them.

There have been numerous times when clients have rationalised not to get rid of colleagues only to have to in the end when the pain became too great and usually after the company has greatly suffered. Irrespective of the situation, you know when another is working against your interests and I am not talking about politicking or credit-seeking. When a change initiative, for example, is derailed because of hidden agenda there is a difference between constructive criticism and guerrilla tactics. 'Work againsts' must go.

'Work fors' accept what they have to do but will not consider alerting you to any difficulties and certainly not when they are unhappy. They will let everyone else know and always have an available ear for others who are also unhappy. Theirs is a form of loyalty but often they are unsure as for what or for whom but they still have a functional role within an organisation. Most of the time they don't say anything about problems because they don't like to get involved; they just want to do the job they receive money in return for doing.

'Work withs' do what they're supposed to do because they want to and because they understand why it is important. Understanding the organisational mission they feel responsible for helping to fulfil it. The people that are within an entrepreneurial leader's remit must be 'work-withs.' They will share their thoughts and ideas and handle yours effectively. Treating work-fors like work-withs can overwhelm them. Conversely, you will offend work-withs by treating them like work-fors. Both are valuable but you need to identify and foster the work-withs because they will develop entrepreneurial attributes under your leadership.

The top ten traits to identify in fostering the right people are:

1. **Chemistry:**
   You will enjoy working with that person
2. **Optimism:**
   They will lift the spirit of your business
3. **Dedication:**
   They will help towards achieving your mission
4. **Enthusiasm:**
   That will grow into a passion for what they do
5. **Compatibility:**
   That will ensure harmony and team strength
6. **Character:**
   A fearlessness to do what ever it takes
7. **Loyalty:**
   To work alongside you through thick and thin
8. **Humorous:**
   The ability to keep things in perspective
9. **Industrious:**
   An abundance of physical and mental energy
10. **Desire:**
    Their energy is fuelled from their commitment

When identifying the right people it is important to develop a clear mental model of the successful candidate. Know exactly the sort of person you are looking for. Too many people rely on the relationship myth that you will know them when you meet them. The fact is that you will recognise them because you know what you are looking for. Too often when you ask another person what they want in a relationship they will be quick to tell you what they don't want. Similarly, you ask another what they are looking for in a job and they will be adamant about what they don't want. What good is that? Be absolutely sure of the people you are looking for and then you will be quick and adamant that they are the right ones.

Remember not to rely on career resumes but ask more personal questions that assist in getting to know the real person. Such questions will help you to rely more on your intuition than on your logic. Remember to be more subjective than objective in your selection. Ultimately you are looking to work with the right people. Anyone can develop the right skills and experience when given the right support. But they must start out with the right traits. Ask any questions that you consider appropriate. Here are just some of the ones I personally use.

1. If you were financially independent what would you do?
2. What do you hope to be doing in five years from now?
3. What is the biggest risk you have ever taken?
4. What movie part would you most like to play?
5. What was the last/best book you read?
6. What TV shows do you like to watch?
7. What is your favourite recreation?
8. What music do you like?
9. What five words do others use when describing you?
10. Why do you want to work here?

There is one final point that I believe inexorably leads to working with the right people. Synchronicity, as coined by Carl Jung, or the happening of a meaningful co-incidence.

On the basis that we attract or gravitate towards what is dominantly held in our mind, which is why we must have a clear picture of what we want and what we are looking for, then the right people will come into our lives at the right time. It is not necessary to intellectually understand why such coincidences happen but it is useful to emotionally expect it. All of us have experienced meeting the right person at the right time and most of us put it down to chance. The fact that it works, however, doesn't mean that we have to understand it. All of us use electricity yet few understand it. We just accept it. What counts is the role it plays in our life.

The right ROLE

One of the functions I am often asked to facilitate is the clarification of people's role. I have always been surprised at how individuals are unclear about their functional position and responsibilities, both at the commencement and implementation. Moreover, often the termination of a position is because the role had not been fulfilled as expected.

Clearly, it is important that people understand what it is they have to do and what is expected of them. It is bizarre that intelligent executives who are supposed to have a sense of personal responsibility do not have role clarity and nor are they able to clarify what is expected of others. What is of vital importance is getting the right people in the right role with the right understanding at the outset, but it is a two way street.

If executives, for example, start a new position and are unclear of their function then they must ask for a detailed clarification. Such clarification must be provided at the beginning. If it is not immediately forthcoming, then the incoming executive must take it that it will probably not be forthcoming and instead prepare a detailed brief on their own and ensure that all appropriate persons are made aware of it. Performing a role on the basis of 'let's see how it goes' is not a good way to start. This is the route of false promises, misguided expectations or misunderstandings.

Developing a detailed document of duties does not mean replacing flexibility with rigidity. That is just an excuse for not having one, because such a detailed brief should include primary, secondary and additional expectations. Shackleton made it clear that, in addition to his men's specific roles within the expedition, there was the expectation to help with all general work and whatever was required in an emergency. That said, even with all the uncertainly of what lay ahead, he still provided written briefs stating exactly their duties and what he expected from each of his crew. He knew that most work relationships fail because of misunderstandings and lack of communicating. Indeed, most job insecurity is related to lack of role clarification.

Every person connected with an organisation either increases or decreases profitability. Some people may have no visible effect on profits, but no effect actually translates into a loss because business about making profit, not treading water. Everyone must know what is expected of them. If you are seeking to recruit, develop and retain the right people then you have to treat them right; and start as you mean for them to continue.

Most families know their roles because of high communication. It is, of course, relatively easy to maintain a family-like atmosphere when a company is small. As the number of personnel increases, however, a corporation tends toward bureaucratization and human relations grow formalised. Sociologists describe such change as moving from a primary group to a secondary group where reason not emotion governs human conduct.

Most job insecurity is related to lack of role clarification

It is possible, however, to create a secondary group composed of many primary sub-groups and maintain communal ties within a functional association. The key is interpersonal relations based on defining roles that people perform with mutual trust and respect. The entrepreneurial leadership of Sam Raynor has turned a family business, Lakeland, into one of the UK's leading home shopping organisations. Working with his two brothers, Martin and Julian, Sam guided the company to pass its first $100m and open 24 leading stores at the time of writing, in addition to its core mail-order products, by applying interpersonal relations based on mutual trust and respect and ensuring that every member has detailed roles.

Award winners for customer service, Lakeland's success is based on continuous in-house training to ensure clarification of what is expected. Despite their growth from local plastic bag supplier to national business with hundreds of exclusive high quality practical products, the camaraderie reflects a warm family atmosphere.

That great entrepreneurial leader, Konosuke Matsushta, applied the same philosophy in his giant corporation renown for having the most consumers. He believed that the understanding of functional responsibilities and mutual trust were vital to keeping harmony and retaining people. Of course, there have to be incentives and rewards but without trust and understanding such elements are worthless. To maintain the primary subgroups he developed business units with people that, even though each unit was treated as a separate company, were all well known to each other. Through periodic transfers from unit to unit close communication was cultivated and a sense of solidarity throughout the organisation.

As an entrepreneurial leader, you must treat your people the way they deserve to be treated. If you are unsure of their role ask them to define their own expectations of it. If it is to be undefined for the purposes of genius expectation then define it as such. For example Bernard Arnault of LVMH (Moet Hennessy Louis Vuitton) the world's most successful purveyor of luxury goods has decentralised his organisation so that each brand runs itself headed by its own artistic director.

The role for John Gallianno, who heads up Dior, is for him to be himself at all times. Any other defined role would inhibit his creative talent but for him the role reminds him to keep performing the function that makes the organisation successful. He is the right person in the right role, which in turn ensures that his attitude for how he performs it will remain right.

Always establish your role, understand what is expected of you but never limit your expectations of yourself.

The right ATTITUDE

A time-honoured approach in finding the right people for the right role is to hire on attitude before aptitude. It will always be possible to train people with the aptitude that is required but it is a hard task to instil the right attitude. Someone with the right attitude is a pleasure to teach and how much he or she knows about the organisation is not important.

Conversely, suppose a person knows your business better than you do, understands the industry exceptionally well and comes to you with a resume that indicates that they are able to carry out exactly want you want them to do, yet they are also adept at seeing negativity, unable to get on with anyone, and quick to complain about everything. Irrespective of credentials, they will very quickly adversely influence your fellow colleagues, customers, prospects, suppliers and whole network similar, to the proverbial bad apple that in time rots the whole barrel.

It takes just one person with a bad attitude to stop the enjoyment of work and successful growth. Remember, the definition of entrepreneurial leadership *involves instilling the confidence to think, behave and act with entrepreneurship in the interests of fully realising the intended purpose of the organisation to the beneficial growth of all stakeholders involved.* Such a worthwhile task should not be derailed because of wrong attitude. However, attitude can be dramatically improved by following personal development and self-evaluation and if you intuitively feel that the person with the bad attitude is worth persevering with, then you must do so because again the best way to learn is to teach. But be careful because one of a manager's biggest mistakes is hiring employees who have less than positive attitudes.

Having the right attitude ensures that the most important role for entrepreneurial leaders, that of developing the ability to see challenges as opportunities and setbacks as temporary inconveniences, is developed to the full. The entrepreneurial leader Herbert Kelleher built Southwest Airlines from a napkin doodle to the most successful airline business ever with a capitalisation bigger than American, United and Continental Airlines combined.

Consistently named as one of best places to work in the US, the company enjoys the industry's highest rate of people retention. But what is most stunning of all about Southwest is that since 1973, when it first turned a profit, the company hasn't lost a penny. In an industry plagued by fare wars, recessions, oil crises, and other disasters, this is an astounding feat. No other airline has ever come close to it. Kellerher maintains that their success is putting the right people in the right role with the right attitude. 'Anyone who looks at things solely in terms of factors that can easily be quantified,' says Kellerher, 'is missing the heart of the business, which is having the right people with the right attitude.'

Chairman Kelleher's and CEO Jim Parkers attitude extends to having a slavish devotion to cash reserves in order that they are able to cope with downturns and not have to resort to layoffs. Both agree that having found people with the right attitude they would not want to lose them. Such a philosophy paid off when the airline industry nose-dived following the terrorist attacks on the World Trade Centre Towers in New York, which historians will mark as one of monumental changes in the 21st Century.

At the time of the disaster Southwest had $1bn in cash reserves. By the next morning they had secured a further $475 million line of credit with banks and had called Boeing Co. to postpone taking 11 more 737s, worth about $30 million apiece, including one that had been scheduled for delivery Sept. 11. While other carriers announced 100,000 layoffs, Southwest avoided job cuts and made a $180 million contribution to its employee retirement plan on schedule on Sept. 14. Even though the very best of attitudes is questioned during such a testing crisis as the world witnessed, it is clear that the right attitude will overcome.

The right COMMUNICATION

I made the point earlier that a person cannot *not* communicate. Whatever their attitude, it will be communicated by as much as what they don't say, as what they do say, because communication is much more than just words. It follows that having the right attitude ensures the right communication. Entrepreneurial leadership cannot function without good open and clear communication lines. In the majority of corporations, however, surveys will invariably highlight poor, closed and vague communication. One of the fundamental impediments to successful growth is that the majority of people do not understand, and therefore do not practice, right communication.

A number of years ago I was involved in a team that developed *TalkWorks*. My client and now friend, BT executive, Adrian Hosford had been instrumental in creating the famous 'it's good to talk' brand and visited me with a view to developing a worthwhile, yet challenging, mission to improve the communicative culture of the UK. Perhaps it was his Irish heritage that allowed him to be a natural communicator but Adrian was ahead of his time when it came to practicing entrepreneurial leadership within an established organisation as British Telecom.

BT's investment, coupled with Adrian and his team, allowed research and development of a program that was able to break down the barriers to, and dramatically improve, communication practice. *TalkWorks* was distributed to millions of customers making it one of the most widely read books of its kind ever published in the UK. It was a unique interactive book because of dedicated 'freefone' lines available for consumers to actually listen to both wrong, and right, communication. Its success was clearly due to illustrating practical applications of simple principles, yet it was because Adrian understood that communicating to his wider consumer audience was the same as communicating to his closer colleagues and friends. He made them feel valued.

Most large companies in the west adopt a communication style that is rooted in the tradition of argumentation and debate. In such a tradition advocacy skills are considered the most important. But another set of skills is often required because such debate and advocacy can impede the flow of ideas. What are required are inquiry skills that are conducive to bringing the best out of everyone involved and are based on the belief that everyone is a valuable source of ideas. Adrian would create a proposal, rather than advocate one, by using vision and values to guide direction and therefore ideas would always flow.

> **The secret central to practicing right communication is making the person you are talking to feel valued.**

In sending a communication Adrian would ensure that you both received and understood it by following it through with requesting what your interpretation of it was and your view as to its application and implementation. This is contrary to the majority of 'unacknowledged' communications that are viewed, by the sender, as being accepted, agreed and understood by the recipient.

Too many corporate communications are based on misunderstanding. Indeed the *TalkWorks* research indicated that when people talk to one another misunderstanding is very common. Either people don't listen or assume what is on another's mind. Eve tells Adam, for example, that she will not be able to attend the executive training course because she has an important client meeting. Eve regrets not being able to attend but the client has priority. Later Adam talks to another colleague, Ruth, and mentions that Eve has found 'a way out of' having to attend the training course, 'or something like that.' When Ruth talks to Eve she mentions that she is 'surprised' by Eve's 'attitude.' Eve feels stung by the rebuke.

---

1. Apply the following to any current project that involves you:

- Are you 100% clear on what your project involves?
- Are you able to articulate its essence in one sentence?
- Are you able to ascertain that others fully understand you?
- Are you able to answer any question relating to it?
- Are you able to sincerely enthuse about it?

2. Apply the following to yourself:

- Do you listen without interruption?
- Do you take on board what others say?
- Do you listen with full attention or 'tune out?'
- Do you advocate proposals or create inquiries?
- Do you consider all ideas that arise from discussion?

3. Ask the following of others:

- How would you rate my attention span when listening to you?
- How would you rate my concentration when in discussion?
- How would you rate my empathy skills, tact and sensitivity?
- How would you rate my patience in talking with you?
- How would you rate the relevance of my input?

Before offering advice as freely as we may have previously done, we need to learn to listen to another without assumptions, prejudices and opinions that each of us carries around with us, waiting for an opportunity to use. This involves learning to listen to our self, acting in the right roles, rather than the roles we adopt in order to please everybody. In this way, we can learn to appreciate where others are coming from. For, without doubt, the secret central to practicing right communication is making the person you are talking to feel valued.

Entrepreneurship demands a high level of awareness. In this way ideas and opportunities are 'tuned' into. As an entrepreneurial leader, therefore, you must practice communication skills because irrespective of how brilliant the ideas and opportunities are they will ultimately be lost, or worthless, unless all communications relating to them are the right ones.

The right TEAMWORK

The right communication is essential for right teamwork. Imagine, for example, that an advance scout sent from a group of pioneers discovers a hostile encampment. If the scout resented being chosen, disliked the pioneer leader and most of the team, he may just decide to bypass the camp and let the group following him fend for themselves. He may, of course, choose to hurry back to the group and warn them, but if the pioneering leader had no confidence in the scout why should he deploy defensive action. If perhaps the leader believes the scout but is unable to organise his people in time to take appropriate action, then the group would be highly vulnerable to slaughter. Of course, should the scout's report be immediately accepted by the leader and acted on by the whole group an alternative route can be successfully embarked upon. It is clearly obvious that for a team to work right it must work as a team. There are three main elements for a team to work right.

First, the whole team working together must be greater than the sum of the individual members. Each member must be chosen because of their strengths and diverse thinking that will compliment other members, and not because they are the best at what they do. A top specialist who prefers to work alone will not make for a good team member. Such a person can be valuable in presenting ideas to a team that will lead to greater effectiveness but 'loners' within a team reduce both their own and the team's effectiveness.

Secondly, a common and shared purpose for the team's existence must be unanimously and enthusiastically bought into. Every team member understands that 'Together Everyone Achieves More' when working towards the same goal. It is alarming how many corporate teams have no clear idea of what their common goal is or indeed their intended function. Teams are there to perform to the best of their ability utilising all of their combined talents on behalf of the organisation that they are part of, and serve. An entrepreneurial team with a specific goal to create value from opportunity should do just that. If it doesn't achieve this goal then the wrong teamwork is involved. It is not that people are wrong, it is more that teams are put together wrong. Entrepreneurial teams must be right or quite simply the creative process and drive that distinguishes them is smothered.

Thirdly, continuous development with reward and recognition are essential for a motivated and effective team. Groups of people that periodically meet to only discuss what is on the agenda are not teams. Right teamwork involves hard work and commitment from every member. In this way, trust and mutual respect are simultaneously strengthened and mistakes are openly and readily discussed because they are viewed as an opportunity to learn and grow. With motivating reward and recognition, agreed by all members and supported by the organisation, the team becomes an exciting place that is conducive to innovation.

It is not that people are wrong, it is that that teams are wrongly put together.

The best teams in sport have coaches consistently ensuring that the above three elements are adhered to. Most teams in business, however, are consistently run more as committees seemingly intent on not being able to act as a team. One team-builder I have enormous respect for is Christopher Cowdray. When I first worked with him he had recently been chosen by the InterContinental Group to develop the Churchill in London into one of the city's leading five-star hotels. It was an enormous challenge as the hotel's reputation had been insidiously going down for years. Though the subject of massive renovation, spending millions of dollars did not make for a five-star hotel alone. What was required was a great team.

Christopher first took the time to choose the executives that he wanted. Such top personnel are hard to come by but Christopher utilised his international network to locate the people that he had either previously worked with, or were exceptional in what they did. Having brought them together, he invested the time and energy in getting them to think as a team with each member fully understanding and accepting what was expected. This team then began to form all the hotel staff into one big team made up of departmental units. Housekeeping would work with engineering where before they had hardly spoken, banqueting liaised with kitchen and security with reception, to the point that all members were pulling in one direction.

BUILDING THE RIGHT TEAM

1. Are you a part of an effective team?
2. Does your team adhere to the 3 elements above?
3. Are you a good team member?
4. How would you describe your team's spirit?
5. Does your team know why it exists?
6. Has your team got the right people?
7. Do the members know their roles?
8. Have all members got the right attitude?
9. Is the communication good, average or poor?
10. Does your team generate innovative ideas?

Irrespective of the department you were dealing with, it was easy to sense the team spirit that Christopher had successfully instilled. The hotel became the success that was hoped for by Intercontinental and was expected by the Churchill Team, and Christopher moved on to head up the Savoy Group's jewel, Claridges. Christopher Cowdray's philosophy in building his team adhered to a sequence similar to the ideas in this chapter: find the right people, explain their role, perform it with the right attitude and communicate the right messages. With such a team in place he was able to develop the right innovation that would attract the customers and ensure the good reputation of the Hotel.

The right INNOVATION

Entrepreneurs innovate; 'comfortable' entrepreneurs do not. Necessity is the mother of invention and the more discomfort the greater the innovation or improvement sought. The frustration and discomfort caused by postal strikes and delays speeded the development of the fax machine. The impractical flimsy fax paper prompted innovation towards the comfort of a practical paper that could be filed, or forwarded. Moving from the fax toward email with electronic attachments, then large documents, then greater speed for the larger complexity of data transferral to voice and data and onward is all about moving from what was once comfortable, but became uncomfortable because of inconvenience, towards comfort once more.

The entrepreneur that first starts a business is in a healthy state of discomfort. As the growing organisation inexorably moves towards a comfortable position in the market it insidiously loses its ability to innovate. It is therefore the role of the entrepreneurial leader to ensure that complacency is replaced with a strategy that is a continuum of moving from discomfort towards comfort.

This is the paradox of practicing the right innovation. Innovation improves the life's comforts, yet it is most effectively nurtured because of life's discomforts. To the degree that either an individual or organisation becomes comfortable is in direct proportion to their inability to innovate. Out-of-box thinking is more successful when individuals are out of their comfort zone. Personally speaking, I have been at my most innovative when the outlook has been bleak. Having taken the time to evaluate my growth and non-growth periods, I discovered an almost direct correlation relating to my discomfort and comfort zones. Now, I consciously take myself out of my comfort zone whenever I feel my creativity waning. Nature has cycles of growth, non-growth, decay and renewal. Man however seeks to grow, then stop when comfortable, later stagnate into complacency and then wonder what on earth he has done to deserve it when something goes wrong. Having got over the shock of losing his comfort he then 'resolves' to do something about it.

> **Innovation improves the life's comforts,
> yet it is nurtured because of discomfort.**

The best ideas are rarely spawned in the office environment. Imagining that he was riding on a beam of light while daydreaming in the sunshine spawned Einstein's theory of relativity, which taking the world beyond Newtonian physics was highly innovative. Swiss engineer George de Mestral while out walking saw the connection between the burrs that stuck to his clothes and a new way of fastening things and spawned Velcro. A new idea is at its most vulnerable during the first few moments of life. In any important relationship, one negative comment outweighs ten positives. Can you imagine if these two had their innovations in the office? They would have been shot down in flames or debated to death.

When attending creative executive retreats I am always frustrated to see how the room has been set up at the planned venue. The hotel, or conference centre, has ensured that 'you make yourself at not at home, but at the office. The office environment along with boardroom setting has been duplicated. With email rooms and mobile telecommunications available at break I wonder what innovations they are going to discuss. With delegates there only in 'body' it is hardly surprising that innovation is so lacking in organisations.

Innovativeness is spawned when out of your comfort zone. Before facilitating to a group of senior managers of Akzo Nobel in Cannes on market innovativeness and entrepreneurship I arranged a minibus to take the participants out of their comfort zone down to a traditional French local market. Giving each person 15 Euros I proposed that they go off on their own and spend it how they wished. I saw them later for a Socratic session at our external amphitheatre at Theseus International Management Institute, and the level of energy and input from all participants was incredible high and many valuable ideas were captured.

On another occasion, I took the executive board out of the 'office away from the office' environment by helicopter and into the rainforest in Brazil where no communications existed. The innovative strategy that was spawned was implemented. On yet another occasion when acting for Bull Systems we visited a bull fighting training ranch. I actually jumped into the ring to fight a real bull to make the point about getting out of our comfort zone. Fortunately I, and the ideas we captured, both survived.

Remembering that what people really want can be concentrated right down to just *good feelings* and *right solutions*; a right innovation is any improvement that fulfils such criteria. Entrepreneurial leaders have a duty to stimulate everyone within their organisation to fulfil such criteria irrespective of the market they are involved with. There is only moving forward or falling behind, there can be no neutral. Companies that stand still are actually falling behind. Innovation is the basis of economic prosperity and entrepreneurship is being innovative. Entrepreneurial corporations must continuously improve through applying out-of-their-comfort-zone-thinking, once more recreating the climate that initially spawned them. Applying the scale of 5 for *really soft* down to 0 for *hard and hungry* answer the following about yourself and your company.

1.	What is your current comfort zone level?
2.	What is your company's current comfort zone?
3.	What is your personal level of creativity?
4.	What is your company's level of innovation?
5.	What is your company's strategy for innovation?

Ensuring regular and right innovation ensures that a business is able to target the right customers.

The right CUSTOMER

For an existing entrepreneurial leader the right customers are those very people that he or she is developing in order to create the entrepreneurial organisation. For the aspiring entrepreneurial leader the right customer is the one that is essential for creating value from maximising the selected opportunity that they are focusing on. In the same way that not every opportunity can be focused on, neither can every customer. It is therefore important to choose the customers on which to prioritise your energy.

Every customer has a different emotional makeup as an individual, and every organisation a different value-driven strategy and all have different problems that need to be solved. You win, and keep, customers by delivering what they want and not what you think they want. Defining the right customer, therefore, requires defining the profile of the person that will ultimately benefit from the added value you create from the right innovation. Put simply, know your customer.

J. W. Marriott, Jr., chairman and president of the customer service focused Hotel Group knew that their first customers were their own people: 'we know that if we treat our people correctly, they'll treat the customers right. And if customers are treated right, they'll come back.' Having the right person in the right role with the right attitude delivering the right communication with the right teamwork to ensure the right innovation will be utterly pointless unless you treat people right.

Treating people wrongly inhibits creativity, confidence, esteem, and generally sends the wrong signals and attitude that pervades a whole organisation. Leaders that do not have time for their people are not leaders. Anyone who is too busy to listen to someone is, in the words of Disraeli: 'inebriated with the verbosity of their own exuberance.

Right customers are those people that you serve because they encapsulate the very raison d'etre of your company. The only way to treat them is right. Generally people will tend to treat others in the way they have been 'conditioned' by the treatment they have received. That is why 'short-termism' of incentive and training programs to improve customer-relation management or innovation, for example, is so fallible.

Any relationship strategy must be consistently and persistently applied by word and deed on a daily basis. If not a 'right customer culture' that has taken years to build can deteriorate within a very short period. For example, years of knowing and treating their internal and external customers right at British Airways were destroyed because leadership altered the focus to a strategy of reducing costs. The intention was not to forget customers but, with the attention on cost reduction, they soon were. When attention moves, intention becomes meaningless. For intention and attention are the bride and groom of right relationships.

The Great Place to Work Trust Index developed by Milton Moskowitz and Robert Levering annually surveys the 'Best companies to Work for.' Whether the companies are small businesses, or multi billion dollar corporations, the central thread of the survey illustrates that 'best companies' leaders persistently communicate the conviction that the contribution of every individual is valued.

Entrepreneurial leaders get the best out of their people and facilitate their growth from employeeship to entrepreneurship when they recognise and treat them as they would the perfect customer. In doing so they are able to ensure that a high, passionate level of energy permeates throughout the whole organisation.

1. Do you treat your people like valued customers?
2. Are you treated like a valued customer at work?
3. Is your attention aligned with your organisation's intention?
4. Is your organisations' intention aligned to customer attention?
5. Does your organisation bring out the best in you?

The right ENERGY

How we are treated directly affects our energy. Every day we have a certain amount of energy: physical, emotional, mental and psychic, in ascending order, with our psychic energy being our most valuable. As our thinking is generally rooted in improving what's wrong, however, the emphasis of our energy is spent in that area.

When the focus of our attention is directed on what we can't do, rather than on what we can do, we drain ourselves of our psychic energy. Beating ourselves up mentally for being bad at something, for example, will consequently cause us to feel mentally perplexed, emotionally frustrated and physically tired. Conversely, praising ourselves for excelling at something will cause us to be mentally stimulated, emotionally euphoric and physically energetic.

The one thing that we all have in common is the amount of time we have in an hour: sixty minutes. Depending on individual priorities the manner in how these same periods are spent are infinite in choice. One thing is certain, however, despite efficient management of time, the majority of our achievements take up only the minority of our time. Using the unit of one hour as a reference point, ten minutes is utilised in channelling our energy proactively; and fifty minutes is wasted in stealing our energy reactively. With the majority of our energy being drained it is of no surprise that there is so much fatigue and depression.

Every waking hour takes us either towards fulfilling our objectives, or away from them. There is no neutral, there is only forwards or backwards. Channelling our energy has nothing to do with keeping in balance, which is more to do with restoring energy that has been drained. When we channel our energy correctly we actually generate energy. Conversely, when we do not, it is diverted into frustration, procrastination and exasperation.

Being in balance means having command over the use of our own energy. This requires spending our time only on those activities that we have previously decided are of high value to us.

Applying the rule of: it is not the hours we put in, it is what each of us put in the hours, and acknowledging that time relates to energy expended, consider how you spend your waking hours:

1. How much time do you spend thinking about what you should have done?
2. How much time do you spend worrying about what you should be doing?
3. How much time do you spend doing things that you couldn't say no to?
4. How much time do you spend doing things that you don't enjoy?
5. How much time do you spend doing things that are interrupted?
6. How much time do you spend doing things you are not very good at?
7. How much time do you spend doing things that are part of a ritual?
8. How much time do you spend doing things that are predictable?
9. How much time do you spend putting off what you have planned to do?
10. How much time do you spend daydreaming about what you want to do?

To argue that spending time, or expending energy, on what you want is just not feasible is unacceptable. However you rationalise it you will not detract from the reality of the way you currently employ your energy. Becoming an entrepreneurial leader requires more than mere discernment.

It demands ruthlessness in saying no to anything that you intuitively feel is draining your energy. This of course requires honesty with yourself as to what is important in your life, for it is only with such honesty that you can be honest with others. Treating others as you yourself would want to be treated, by definition involves thinking of what is right for you first, for when you are on course your increased energy is beneficial to others.

There is nothing more personally motivating, more energy building, more fulfilling and more worthwhile, than knowing that what you do is what is important to you, holds meaning for you, is what you want to do, and, above all, is what you are inclined to do. Each of us is pure energy and it is our personal responsibility as to how we direct our energy. If we allow others to drain our energy, then we must accept responsibility for allowing it to happen. Similarly, whenever we involve ourselves in something that is of no interest to us, we must be aware that we are not channelling our energy effectively.

Entrepreneurs have a high level of energy because they are chasing their passion and they must channel effectively to be successful. Entrepreneurial leaders naturally raise the energy levels of people within an organisation because they ensure people are able to focus on what they are best at.

> **We must accept responsibility for letting others drain our energy.**

For example, the President of The Carrier Corporation, Geraud Darnis, consistently ensures that the right people do what they are good at. Because he believes that such a policy ensures that the right energy, a high level, will radiate throughout The Carrier Corporation, which is a company that measurably improves the quality of people's lives. From the time the entrepreneurial founder, Willis Carrier, invented the basics of modern air conditioning in 1902, Carrier has been the world leader in the manufacturer of air conditioning, heating and refrigeration equipment for commercial, residential and transportation applications.

When you buy food from supermarket refrigeration units, or enter into air-conditioned hotels, offices, libraries or museums Carrier will more than likely have been instrumental in providing the right environment. With over 45,000 people in over 170 countries ensuring the right innovations go into the right products and services it is important that there is the right energy, particularly at leadership level.

Working with Geraud is a pleasure because in addition to walking his talk he has learned to know exactly where and when to channel his energy most effectively. At one of his leadership events he shared with me how he had learned that it was possible to achieve much more in less time through greater focus. He said that: 'knowing what your objectives are and why they should be achieved coupled with actually wanting and expecting to achieve them stimulates your energy.'

Energy is always higher when what you have to do is what you want to do. In tapping the right energy you are able to fend off energy draining distractions. People, however, will gravitate toward you because of your high energy. Many will want you to support them in their own endeavours because of your energy. In turn, when you support what is in harmony with your own values and objectives energy increases further. Similarly, when someone else who believes in your objectives supports you, energy increases. It is therefore important to discern what is the right support and practice giving and receiving it.

The right SUPPORT

Practicing giving and receiving support is fundamental for entrepreneurship. Without the right support all ventures and adventures will fall down. Without the moral support of my wife and children I would not have considered undertaking what I have in the past or will yet do in the future. Soon after starting my first business, supportive mentors helped me through those inevitable times when confidence is low. Without the support from funding sources either bank mangers or investment brokers I would not have been able to expand any of my businesses. Without the support of a network of customers, suppliers and associations there would have been little success. I am also sure that the support that I have in turn provided, either in morale, advice or financial terms, has been the right support at the time.

Without support from parents, teachers, career advisors, children have a tough time – which no parent should want. There must always be the right support to ensure that an individual's potential is released to the full. Similarly there must always be the right support systems to create entrepreneurial organisations.

The first of the six core characteristics essential for an organisation to develop, discussed in chapter 2, was: Agreed Support Strategy. Learning the principles and applying the practices of entrepreneurial leadership in order to develop entrepreneurial attributes, pursue selected opportunities, and drive through ventures will be doomed to failure before even starting, without the right support strategy. Establishing support sponsors, support groups and support systems is integral in creating an entrepreneurial organisation's culture. This leads us into: 'Service v Structure.'

Part Three:
Service v Structure

Chapter 5
Creating an Entrepreneurial People Culture

Chapter 6
Creating an Entrepreneurial Customer Ethos

Chapter 7
Creating Entrepreneurial Opportunities

Chapter 5
Creating an Entrepreneurial People Culture

PEOPLE THAT HAVE ENTREPRENEURIAL INCLINATIONS within established organisations often consider, wish or desire to run their own business. Most of them don't because of comfort, habit and concerns over job security. Having asked countless executives what they would do if money was no object the majority of them have confided that they would like to run their own business. These individuals, I believe, are invaluable to creating the successful organisation of the 21st Century: the entrepreneurial organisation. The business entrepreneur may have enjoyed success over the past century but now it is the era of the life entrepreneur: those who want command over their lives.

These entrepreneurial individuals will expect that the organisation they are part of will fulfil their needs and aspirations in return for fulfilling strategic corporate aspirations. Such reciprocity demands a paradigm shift in organisational and management traditional thinking.

Having evolved from a manufacturing-driven to a market-driven and then on to a customer-driven paradigm, the challenge for business must now be to move to a relationship-driven paradigm that is responsive to the needs and aspirations of both customers *and* employees equally. Such a challenge demands that corporate structures are customised with greater flexibility towards employees and accordingly attracts, develops and retains both them and customers. Existing structures can be adapted to function this way by harnessing the immense experience and data acquired because of the customer-driven paradigm.

Copowerment

In the same way that the customer-driven paradigm recognised that customer demands could not be viewed as an annoying impediment to neat organised control systems; the relationship-driven paradigm will recognise that empowerment is no longer the powerful tool for growth it was originally considered to be.

To have power from one 'superior' source delegated to a 'subordinate' source does not release potential to take ownership, be creative, or think entrepreneurially. The evolving life entrepreneurs will no longer expect to be treated as 'tools' but as entities of the business. Such expectations will have to be fulfilled through *copowerment*: where both management and people share and exercise power for common purpose.

Where structure has traditionally been influenced by a pre-determined fixed strategy, a service oriented copowerment structure will provide the much-needed balance between what is important for organisations and what is important for individuals. This will achieve the much sought after, yet elusive, alignment between organisations and the individuals that make them up. This, in turn, is the essential key to instilling the vital sense of ownership and entrepreneurship that all future corporations must become endowed with in order to grow successfully. Such a practical concept of alignment relies on trust, the very foundation on which relationship-driven companies are built.

Creating a corporate entrepreneurial culture involves 'growing' reciprocal trust within an agile organisation where copowerment is not restricted by boundaries. In a relationship-driven business people are not managed, they are treated as trustworthy individuals that willingly commit their time, and energy, into what they want to do and have to do. Because they understand that there are no boundaries between the two. Such a customised structure will require both commitment and accountability from employees. Clearly, there must be shared ownership and indeed real entrepreneurial leaders consider such commitment as a prerequisite to starting, or investing in, a business.

Establishing Entrepreneurial Leadership Learning

For copowerment to be effective, people must develop the trust and confidence that they are working together as valuable 'business owners' towards success. Confidence and trust are best established through mutual support and reciprocal mentoring of individuals while applying the principles and practices of entrepreneurial leadership. Trust and confidence may be honed when times are difficult because the qualities are tested. But they are best developed through good times in the same way that a honeymoon period helps bond a new relationship of mutual commitment.

The difficulty is that most organisations get involved in addressing cultural change more because of reducing the 'pain' rather than seeking the benefits of the 'pleasure' derived from improved culture. For that reason when an company makes a strategic decision to become entrepreneurial it must adapt its structure towards one that ensures continuous learning, clarification of aspirations, and consistent flexibility to change.

The responsibility for taking action lies with the existing, established leadership of the organisation and can never be delegated. 'Aspiring' entrepreneurial leaders must engage in establishing the template of what they want, no matter how long it takes, through co-mentoring and copowerment with each other. In my own experience, change processes that fail, particularly in large and established organisations, are due to a lack of definite action by existing leadership.

Leaders are still human beings and many are often unaware that change is required. Often they resist change because they feel secure 'with the way things are around here' and unfortunately they have the influence to make certain that things do remain the 'comfortable' way. Indeed, one of the first symptoms for change is a distinct lack of innovation because a business becomes stuck in a comfort zone.

Leadership mentors develop greater understanding and team spirit between colleagues. Mentoring leadership does not mean acting as a counsellor. It involves starting where colleagues are with a view to taking them where it is best for the organisation to go. Learning must start, continue and be never-ending at leadership level. The long-term objective is to develop a culture of entrepreneurial leaders at all levels. To ensure that such leaders become effective change champions, the ultimate example of what is expected must be consistently set.

Establishing an entrepreneurial learning culture starts with every individual at leadership level immersing themselves in personal evaluation and then 360-degree feedback with their colleagues. Next is ensuring that the leadership team fills the criterion of being diverse and working together with openness and trust; each colleague co-mentors the other. Concurrent with this process, and indeed part of it, is to develop the 'draft proposal' of vision, mission and strategy: revisiting what the corporation exists for, what its primary objective to achieve is, and how it is going to go about it. Cultivating the basics as explained in chapter 1 is the sequence to follow.

When this process had been successful, irrespective of how long it takes, the 'draft proposal' is ready to be communicated and duplicated. Though having a deadline galvanises the process into progressing, it is not so important how long the process takes, as it is to have team unanimity.

One of the hurdles to overcome at Pfizer UK, and one that is common in large companies, was to attain such unanimity. It took longer than expected simply because members perceived things differently. Eventually achieving the unanimity, however, was a decisive factor in the success of communicating the 'draft proposal.' I refer to 'draft' because it is impossible to win the hearts and minds of others if what you want is already set in stone. Involvement can transform into commitment when others are copowered to develop together. Though the draft proposal did not alter much over the course of its yearlong period, before being unanimously supported to become 'real,' it sent the right signal that what was required was everyone's support.

> **Diverse unanimity harnesses complementary strengths of leaders into a unified purpose.**

Leading people is always about leading change and bringing the best out in them and ourselves. Resisting change is about our search for control and predictability in our lives, which does not bring out the best in us. Both involve learning continuously about others and ourselves however. The more we learn about what we want and our capabilities, the more our natural entrepreneurship will come to our aid.

In revisiting the definition of Entrepreneurial Leadership that *'involves instilling the confidence to think, behave and act with entrepreneurship in the interests of fully realising the intended purpose of the organisation to the beneficial growth of all stakeholders involved;'* it is clear that winning the hearts, minds and entrepreneurial spirits of people is a process of never-ending learning through application and duplication. Leadership and strategy must establish an entrepreneurial learning culture in order that entrepreneurial initiatives, essential for growth, are willingly sponsored.

An argument often raised is that it is not possible to have a diverse team that operates unanimously in implementing major strategy. My response is that diverse unanimity harnesses complementary strengths into unified purpose. With such leadership focus success is certain. Inevitably, where there is a continuous lack of unanimity, board members unable to get on board mentally and emotionally might have to leave physically.

Sponsoring Entrepreneurial Initiatives

When the leadership team have unanimously committed the organisation to becoming entrepreneurial, established an agreed support strategy and taken the time to communicate the intention throughout, then the sponsoring of entrepreneurial initiatives can commence. These 'laboratories' provide the environment for developing the six core characteristics of entrepreneurship as discussed in Chapter 2. Most established organisations operate under centralised leadership. Decentralised separate business units therefore should be established under the direction of an appointed, yet willing, sponsor to support these initiatives.

Once a test business unit has been established entrepreneurial 'willing' champions need to be identified and selected to operate it. These entrepreneurs, as they should be termed, must have a good relationship with the sponsor in terms of mentoring support and copowerment. Their 'practical' training will take the form of identifying and pursuing selected opportunities within understood markets and obtaining the required resources to develop, and implement, the appropriate business plan.

This mentoring, sponsoring and copowering are important in supporting these entrepreneurs in the new business units. The sponsor/mentor provides a resource and outlet for entrepreneurial development and learning and ensures that the six core characteristics are consistently and beneficially applied. At the same time the sponsor must ask themselves self certain questions to confirm that they are fulfilling their role as intended:

1. Am I supporting the six core entrepreneurship characteristics?
2. What entrepreneurial initiative has been proposed?
3. How am I mentoring the champions and sponsoring the initiative?
4. Will the allocation of resources be sufficient for the initiative?
5. Have I confirmed that a sequential planning process is clarified?
6. Is the copowerment effectively monitoring the initiative?
7. Am I removing obstacles from the initiative's developmental path?
8. Have I defined the parameters of what must be accomplished?
9. What recovery plans are there if the initiative is unsuccessful?
10. Did the initiative have alignment with our agreed strategy?

CORE ENTREPRENEURSHIP CHARACTERISTICS	
Employee	**Organisational**
1. Decisive Personal Choice	Agreed Support Strategy
2. Design, Develop, Drive & Determine	Provide Initiative Sponsorship
3. Willingly risk moderate failure	Establish Trial & Error Metrics
4. Interdependent Member	Encourage Multi-disciplined Teams
5. Define Project Expectations	Allocate Venture Resources
6. Concept Value Recognition	Performance & Risk Reward

Table 5.1

The idea of a decentralised unit is to create the environment that is conducive to stimulating entrepreneurial thinking and entrepreneurial leadership. A stimulating entrepreneurial culture will clearly motivate and develop the desired entrepreneurial behaviour and characteristics effectively. Indeed, there is a proven correlation between smaller unit size and entrepreneurial behaviour. The diversified giant 3M with its 4,000 profit centres, for example, are more like a living organism than an organisation.

What is of vital importance for the ultimate success of separate units is that the sponsor, leader or manager that drives the team must be an entrepreneurial leader in mind and spirit in order to facilitate the right environment and lead by example. Their influence, support and expertise, will ultimately prove to be instrumental in the unit's success and growth into a larger and more profitable enterprise.

OILing Decentralised Entrepreneurial Units

The basic rule introduced by former chairman William L. McKnight of the $15bn organisation, 3M, encapsulates how decentralised entrepreneurial units should ideally operate:

'As business grows, it becomes increasingly necessary to delegate responsibility and to encourage men and women to exercise their initiative. This requires considerable tolerance. Those men, and women, to whom we delegate authority and responsibility, if they are good people, are going to want to do their job in their own way. Mistakes will be made. But if a person is essentially right, the mistakes he or she makes are not as serious in the long run as the mistakes management will make if it undertakes to tell those in authority exactly how they must do their jobs. Management that is destructively critical when mistakes are made kills initiative. And it's essential that we have many people with initiative if we are to continue to grow.'

In chapter 2 the point was made that Opportunity-focused, Innovation-driven Leadership (OIL) must be in abundance for entrepreneurial success. Communicating an opportunity or innovation initiative to gain sponsorship relies on contagious enthusiasm. Getting colleagues to support new lines of research depends both on hard work and a willingness to explain the new possibilities you see. Once support is obtained, persistence then becomes a team effort.

The objective of business unit leader, John Moon, for example, was the creation of a 3M proprietary technology that could perform in extreme temperatures and stick to a range of surfaces. Moon's ability to win both respect and affection from his colleagues helped him to champion his initiative and lead the commercialisation effort. He credits the success of his unit to the sponsorship he received, and such confidence in Moon paid off. Research and dedication to expand the technology platform has led to a large family of innovative products that represent hundreds of millions of dollars in global sales for 3M.

This approach has rewarded 3M with thousands of supported initiatives. Under the principle of 'grow and divide' small units founded on innovation and entrepreneurship are encouraged to grow into larger divisions. Indeed 3M encourage its people to devote 15% of their time to independent projects that could lead to being developed under a sponsored initiative. The 'defined project expectations' coupled with 'allocating venture resources' ensures that 25% of each units' sales is actually generated from products within five years of being initiated.

Clearly, it is the responsibility and role of the entrepreneurial business unit leader to structure and organise the unit so that as it grows it does not attract the inevitable non-entrepreneurial regulations and bureaucratic obstacles commonly associated with large corporations. To set up decentralised, flat, non-hierarchal entrepreneurial units that begin to arrange themselves into rigid pyramids would be self-defeating, yet this can quite quickly happen. And usually it is when the entrepreneurial business unit manager moves on and is replaced by another that was not involved in creating the unit's environment. Once again, when focus changes, a whole environment can be adversely affected unless the cultivation of the basics and the sequence of the six core characteristics are followed.

> **Entrepreneurial leaders use copowerment to ensure that decision-making and ownership are close to both market and customer.**

The ideal business unit must be flat and liberally OILed. In this way, it benefits from its closeness to both market and customers. For this is where its entrepreneurial personnel pursue their selected opportunities and are stimulated to develop innovations to create added value for the organisation. The entrepreneurial business unit leader must copower his or her unit by ensuring that decision-making and ownership are the closest possible to both market and customer, which is why the unit was set up to create value from initiative in the first place.

Driving Entrepreneurial Venture Teams

The following points clarify entrepreneurial teams.

- Entrepreneurship is an activity that creates value and is most effective when applied in a team that starts a new venture motivated by a stimulating market opportunity that has been identified to pursue.

- It is the quality of an entrepreneurial team that is the

determinant success factor in highly profitable ventures. An entrepreneurial team will initially comprise the founding members of a start-up company or 'sponsored' business unit.

- It is important that the team is added to with additional increasing strength and knowledge similar to the layers of an onion. It is the role of the entrepreneurial leader to blend and grow these layers into an integrated working team.

- The catalyst to stimulate the right team into right action is of course the right venture. Such value creation is their reason for being.

- Diverse thinking, complementary strengths, unanimity for dominant purpose are essential for the right team as are the blending of management and entrepreneurial skills.

- Loyalty and trust within the team, effectiveness of group decision making, commitment to agreed objectives and understanding of customer needs and market trends.

Forming and developing the right entrepreneurial team takes time of course, particularly because individual team members need to understand their own self-awareness, the team awareness and the strategic awareness of the organisation they are part of, or that is sponsoring them as a business unit. Team members must develop in each other the entrepreneurial qualities of:

- becoming aware, keeping alert and staying proactive
- understanding the role of capturing the value of uncertainty
- determining and developing market trends and voids
- selecting and focusing on their opportunities
- designing their unit structure and systems accordingly
- committing to persistently drive through chosen ventures
- focusing specifically while maintaining agility
- engaging the energies of their entire network
- become enthusiastic communicators
- accepting that mistakes are a measure of success

Above all, however, an entrepreneurial team must not get bogged down with distracting issues and minutiae, as the moment it does it ceases to operate either effectively or entrepreneurially. The venture therefore must be highly motivating and be able to fully absorb the interests of team members. One of the challenges in ensuring the success of business units is getting teams together. It is not necessary that a team is together all the time, indeed some of the best teams may meet only periodically while doing the appropriate work required of them. But there should never be any difficulty in bringing them together when it is required. If there is, then the team and the venture realities and commitments must be revisited.

Quite simply, any sponsored business unit must come into existence because an aspiring entrepreneurial leader is passionate about driving through their selected initiative. An organisation that identifies an initiative only to delegate it to a business unit without the buy-in of the unit's personnel is already on the road to failure. This is clearly not a rule of thumb, but it is true to say that I have witnessed many initiatives fail where the only incentive has been competitor-driven rather than commitment-driven.

Traditional organisational teams where projects are delegated to impassionate personnel and are driven by traditional methods of remuneration and even performance bonus can of course be successful. But the most important part about entrepreneurial ventures is that by the very nature of them, when they are successful they are significantly more profitable than traditional ventures. That is why large established corporations must look to recreate as entrepreneurial ones.

Clearly companies such as Microsoft to Matsushita and GE to IBM have recognised increasingly that the real value of sponsoring business units is that it is conducive to involving the entrepreneurial team that is committed to pursuing initiatives. A lesser known example, however, is the South African 'state-owned' Industrial Development Corporation (IDC).

Established in 1940, the IDC, having undergone major remodelling, today operates with an entrepreneurial strategy that ensures all its sponsored ventures are driven by passionate involved teams. The vision of the IDC is to be the primary driving force of commercially sustainable industrial development and innovation to the benefit of South and southern Africa. Its mission is to promote entrepreneurship through the building, organisational collaboration and sponsoring of initiatives based on entrepreneurial principles and practices. Even though state-owned it is self-financing, through the success of its sponsored initiatives, and functions as a private enterprise.

As it approached its 60th year in 2000, IDC made a strategic decision to redefine its mission and undergo the substantial change required to become entrepreneurial. It reduced its hierarchical levels from seven to four, providing for a more flexible and flatter structure, and organised its operations into strategic business units to ensure industry-specific focus and delivery of high-quality, innovative service to clients. Designing the organisational chart around key decision processes optimised decision-making and, most importantly, the process involved the development of teams with clearly assigned accountability. Its core strategy to identify and support opportunities, not yet addressed by the market, could then be effectively implemented by these teams within the opportunity-focused, yet industry-specific, business units.

With entrepreneurial initiatives ranging from mining to tourism, textiles to agro industries and chemicals to finance IDC was soon able to invest upwards of $500m annually in further entrepreneurial initiatives. One IDC initiative is aimed at emerging industrialists interested in acquiring small to medium sized ventures with entrepreneurial venture teams that are prepared to play a meaningful role in managing the business and are committed to making a cash contribution of at least 10% of the purchase price. South Africa's third largest gold producer, Harmony Gold Mining, for example, became the first real 'copowerment' initiative in the gold mining industry. IDC is successful because its strategic business units comprise entrepreneurial-minded teams able to specifically advise on sought out selected initiatives. When compiling a team for a specific venture the criteria in selecting members to work together beyond those mentioned above are:

- Does the candidate have experience in the specific industry?
- Have they a proven competency record for entrepreneurial initiatives?
- Will they have credibility in the industry and with team colleagues?
- Are they compatible with the team, unit and corporate culture?
- What network or resources are they bringing to the team?
- Are they motivated to be part of the team, unit and initiative drive?

Rewarding Entrepreneurial Behavior

The first part of the Entrepreneurial Organisations' definition is: *'promote entrepreneurial activity.'* Encouraging the right people to act in the right roles with an entrepreneurial attitude to create value from opportunity must be founded on a reward system that is meaningful and motivating. To bring the very best out in people it is important to reward people as they expect and as they don't expect. Finding out what their 'hot button' is, and turning it on, develops commitment and creativity.

Twenty years ago I rewarded an employee of mine in such an unexpected way that it even surprised me. An exclusive cocktail bar, restaurant and nightclub of which I was part owner had been full every night. I was delighted and while visiting the venue could see that our choice of bar manager had been absolutely right. People love to be made welcome and he would remember their names, drinks and serve them with great panache. To my surprise, however, despite the wealth of both customers and clientele, stock levels were not reducing accordingly and revenue did not relate to the huge amount of customers. Puzzled as to why this was happening I visited the club early one evening and discovered the bar manager restocking the bar from his own vehicle with stock that he had purchased himself. By selling his own liquor, and keeping the money, the club's inventory remained unaffected.

Caught in the act he admitted to outright theft. Irrespective of his genuine personal mitigating circumstances such a betrayal of trust should really have resulted in immediate dismissal, with a view to criminal charges being brought. Unexpectedly for him, however, I chose to entertain a different course of action. I invited him to purchase shares in the club and doubled his salary in order that he could do so.

The entrepreneurial ideas he had already applied were making the club renown and I believed that if he could apply all his energies, flair and commitment, as a 'business owner' the business would benefit. Perhaps the business psychologist in me was persuaded into doing such a 'test,' yet the change in the man was incredible as were the fortunes of the business.

Admittedly, this is a highly unusual example but I share it to illustrate the power of believing in another and trusting them even when they know they don't deserve your trust. Sometimes people are driven to be dishonest when they would be better off using those same energies to address a problem, rather to try and get around it in the hope that it might go away. Whatever the reason when given another chance the commitment from the individual will be stronger than ever.

This is important because the nature of developing entrepreneurial behaviour involves making mistakes, even costly ones. But even though they may lead to failure, certain actions should sometimes be rewarded. In doing so it builds the courage to risk and follow things through. Remember, every large organisation came into being because people that had the courage of their convictions and followed their commitments through overcame mistakes and failure.

Take every opportunity to visibly display to colleagues, partners and teams that you believe in them and have trust in their ability. Trust begets trust and value creation from opportunity results. It is often worth keeping a daily praise and criticism note in your diary. Most people unfortunately spend more time criticising than praising. A praiseworthy email or letter is revisited and the recipient feels that his or her ship has come in. Conversely, a thoughtless email or letter may be quickly deleted or destroyed, yet harbours in the mind for ever. Statues only exist for those individuals that have been criticised, never for the critics. Ask yourself regularly, is your behaviour towards other people dampening the entrepreneurial behaviour so essential to your organisation?

> **Trust begets trust resulting in
> value creation from opportunity.**

The fundamental reward for entrepreneurial behaviour is the same as the motivator for instilling and developing it: ownership. Entrepreneurial organisations must comprise people that have a personal stake. Not every one wants to be an entrepreneur nor wants to have their entrepreneurial attributes brought out. Similarly, not every one will want to take up the opportunity to have stock or share ownership. But to the degree that there is not either the opportunity or the interest for 'ownership' will be proportionate to how much an organisation will not be entrepreneurial. Similar to entrepreneurial leader, Jim Clark, I will only ever invest in businesses that reward 'taking ownership behaviour' with ownership. Moreover, the corporation that does not ensure that the majority of its people have a vested interest is not entrepreneurial and will not be able to benefit from the value that such entrepreneurship creates.

Wal-Mart is arguably the most successful business in US. Its entrepreneurial leader, Sam Walton, consistently applied the reward related rule of: Share your profits with all your associates and treat them as partners. In turn, they will treat you as a partner and together you will all perform beyond your wildest expectations. Remain a corporation and retain control if you like, but behave as a servant leader in partnership. Encourage your associates to hold a stake in the company. Reward them with discounted stock for their retirement. As Walton said: 'It's the single best thing we ever did.'

Chapter 6
Creating an Entrepreneurial Customer Ethos

NON-ENTREPRENEURIAL ORGANISATIONS continue to *spend* huge finance budgets on marketing, without really listening. Entrepreneurial organisations *invest* their time, energy and imagination in listening to, and understanding, customers. Irrespective of the size or age of a company today, future success and growth tomorrow is relative to being entrepreneurial and establishing a customer ethos.

The days of *'it's a numbers game'*; *'next;'* *'love 'em and leave em;'* *'and there'll be more where they came from,'* are over. As is the marketing textbook adage: that customers know what they want, you just have to supply it. Because customers neither want to be treated like a transaction, nor do they know in advance exactly what they want. A customer-focused ethos involves imagining what the future holds, perceiving how market trends will shift, anticipating what the demand will be and proactively raising the awareness of customers, thereby actually creating and becoming the future.

Entrepreneurship is about creating, implementing, driving and following through an innovative idea that seeks to maximise value from opportunity. The hard fact is, however, that with customer awareness, competition intensity and less brand loyalty the 'innovative idea that seeks to maximise value from opportunity' is increasingly hard to bring to market and more often than not fails. The software industry, for example, has experienced a failure rate as high as 90% during some periods of its history.

In addition to this, having moved from a product-selling and customer-quantity paradigm to one of customer-serving and being relationship-driven, it is now more important than ever to know: who the customer you want to serve is; what level of relationship will develop loyalty with you; why they will want to do business with your company; and how you will attract, lead and educate them to raise their expectations and perceptions as to how your product or service will beneficially serve them.

Clarifying the Customer and Market

Marketing focus is leaning increasingly inward to existing customers, as opposed to outward strangers. Cultivating and growing a customer base must involve getting to know them well in order to market to them effectively but it is, of course, vital that you clarify what market you are entering and establish the customer profile that your market comprises.

A paradox of the global accessibility is that markets are splitting into more and more niches. As they do, of course, customers become even more important, and they know it. It is vital, therefore, to know the market. Most start-up entrepreneurs get to know their market because it is local to them. For the entrepreneurial corporation this luxury is not always available so it is important that entrepreneurial business units take on a partner, or team member, that does know the 'local' market as well as researching thoroughly at street level.

	Non-Entrepreneurial	Entrepreneurial
1.	Marketing strategy	Customer-focused ethos
2.	Market size	Market niche
3.	Customer quantity	Customer perception
4.	Meet customer needs	Anticipate customer wants
5.	Improve service for market	Create service with customer
6.	Generalised products	Customised convenience
7.	Quality imitation	Desired innovation
8.	Customer relationship	Customer partnership
9.	Know competitors' strengths	Understand competitors' mistakes
10.	External market data	Close customer communication
11.	Global scope, local focus	Global identity, personal service
12.	Market duration	Speed to market
13.	Market leader	Niche diversity
14.	Marketing review	Follow-up service
15.	Research related	Feedback reflective

This involves visiting and getting to know the people you are targeting and then evaluating and reflecting on the research you collate. Such clarification requires a shift in thinking about both customer and market. There are specifically 15 factors that I have identified in order to distinguish the non-entrepreneurial organisation of today from the entrepreneurial organisation tomorrow in marketing and customer related criteria as listed in the box on page 223.

Entrepreneurial leaders Richard Branson of Virgin and Jeff Bezos of Amazon both apply entrepreneurial criteria similar to the above right hand column. Each criterion forces a different paradigm and all encapsulate the competitive advantage entrepreneurial organisations have. Particularly important factors are speed, convenience and follow-up.

Bezos was more interested in providing a fast, convenient, repeat service than selling cheap books. If you live in a town centre and have time on your hands to enjoy a coffee while browsing a Barnes & Noble or Waterstones bookstore that's just great. But if you don't then allocating the time to travel to the store, getting there, looking for what you want, queuing to be served if you can't find it and then waiting for it to come in if you have to order it and phoning to see if it has come in and then returning to the store can be inconvenient and time consuming.

Being recognised as a valued customer and being offered books that similar purchases have indicated may interest you fulfils customer criteria of speed, convenience and follow-up service. The customer feels a valued partner in deciding what offerings are available. The customer may not be aware of what he or she actually wants to read next, but the follow-up service provides guidance and suggestion on a 'why not go for it' basis, rather than 'why have it' or 'do you really need it?' basis.

Branson's Virgin Atlantic, similar to other businesses that operate under the Virgin brand, diversifies into further niche markets by creating an experience rather than just a sale. An executive taking a flight can be collected from home and taken on to a hotel before and after a flight respectively, after having enjoyed various home comforts on board which will soon include hotel and restaurant facilities. The traveller is considered a valued guest, even family member and enjoys, once again, speed, convenience and follow-up service. Ask yourself:

- Does your company have a customer-focused ethos?
- Is there clarification of who your customer is?
- Has your market been clearly determined?
- Are you able to anticipate future niche markets?
- Is your customer perceived as a long-term partner?
- Does your customer perceive your service as fast and convenience?
- Do you perceive 'follow-up' as the start of a relationship?

Serving profitably beyond the brief

I have never forgotten a piece of advice given to me by a former school friend, almost 30 years ago, soon after I had started my first 'full-time' job: 'Never do more than you are paid for.' Fortunately, I have never heeded it. I felt such advice was misguided at the time, even though it was suggested because of my workload, and I still find it impossible to any make sense of today. My preferred axiom is to *always* do considerably more than what you are paid for. Yet, during my business, and professional, career I have discovered that most people habitually provide the minimum rather than the maximum. Unfortunately, over-promising and under-delivering is the norm both from a marketing and a customer service perspective.

> **Entrepreneurship involves serving customers profitably; traditional business too often involves doing just a job.**

Entrepreneurial corporations must not be concerned about receiving a day's work for a day's wages. Its success will depend on what you are able to deliver, not promise or are qualified to do.

When the 19th-century painter Whistler was taken to court, because the client thought the sketch fee excessive, the judge asked how long it took to draw. '10 minutes and a lifetime of experience,' the artist replied. Entrepreneurial leadership requires more than a person's hands, brain and time. It demands creative artistry, abundant energy, out of box imagination, and a willing spirit as well as:

Insight to anticipate future market trends and customer needs; being
Intuitive in deciding how to act on such trends and needs; acting with
Initiative to effectively maximise the opportunities that arise; being
Innovative in creating value from such opportunity; having
Integrity to ensure such opportunity is meaningful and worthwhile; and
Individuality for readily accepting ownership; with
Interdependence to drive initiatives with teamwork.

Entrepreneurship involves serving customers profitably with all the above skills; traditional business tends to involve following a remit. This age of the knowledge-worker means working with your knowledge, not just having knowledge of your work. Exceptional professionals are rare because they apply their knowledge meaningfully towards a worthwhile end. The accountant that fills in your tax return satisfactorily is not providing a service; he or she is doing a job. But the entrepreneurial accountant that suggests creative ways to increase your disposable income, and thus improve your quality of life, is providing a service.

The dentist that removes the decayed tooth is doing a job. The entrepreneurial dentist that suggests specific restorative methods that will significantly improve your confidence is providing a service. The business consultant that does exactly what is expected of him or her is doing a job. The entrepreneurial consultant that proposes an innovative idea, and explains how to follow it through to lead to improved revenue and quality of work environment is providing a service. All the former in the three examples are fulfilling a remit. The latter are serving profitably beyond the brief. All stakeholders must receive benefit from such action.

Learning to pay complete attention to customers is the key for developing customer loyalty. The biggest challenge for everyone involved in service has got to be to keep their mind on the person they are either serving, or are there to serve. People are just not trained to do so. Sometimes, they are entirely unaware of the customer before them. No one likes to be ignored but when you ignore a customer you might as well just dehumanise them.

It is on those rare occasions when you meet someone who genuinely pays you attention that you feel terrific. You spend the whole day feeling good, simply because another person has emotionally energised you with their sincere and full attention. Remember people don't want to be sold to, but they like buying. And they buy people not things. That's what develops customer loyalty. Genuinely making them feel good for buying from you and by serving them with the solutions that they want. Such a business can only grow in strength, both in customers and reputation.

Chief operating officer, David Pottruck of the broker Charles Schwab applied the above philosophy ensuring benefit was enjoyed by all. Charles Schwab's success was founded on having developed a rich network of relationships. The rise of the internet offered great accessibility for clients and, for those not concerned about a personal service, was very reasonable with the broker charging just $29 a trade. The difficulty was that those clients where the serious money came from understandably wanted a dialog and were charged a much higher rate. Pottruck saw that such a dichotomy could lead to losing these clients. Serving clients fully with just a single tier at just $29 a trade, however, would depress the company's earnings by at least 20%; $100m.

> **Serving profitably beyond the brief is a defining element of blending entrepreneurial leadership and experienced management skills together.**

The founder Charles Schwab had a guiding principle that insisted on putting the customer first. But before taking the strategic decision he wanted the fullest analysis culminating in how soon the benefit from such action would be reached. Pottruck produced and, as predicted within the first quarter of the broker announcing that it was offering web trading at just $29 a time and extending all service to all customers, revenue dived. Yet, the insight that the share transactions were moving to the web was proved right. Within 18 months online customers had doubled and profits rose almost 30%. The relationship of trust and confidence between the founder and the executive board was very much a deciding factor in Pottruck initiative in 'doing more than his job's worth.'

Serving profitably beyond the brief is a defining element of blending entrepreneurial leadership and experienced management skills together. Leaders and executive teams must copower people by valuing and making use of the initiatives proposed. Personal ownership in the company coupled with copowerment and interdependence ensures a firm relationship bond based on information flow and respect, it also ensures that service wins over structure every time.

Structure can always be adapted, changed or redesigned, instilling the desire to search consistently for innovative ways to serve profitably beyond what is expected. It does exist within and must be nurtured. For it is without doubt the most important factor for providing value to all stakeholders in business.

Doing more than expected is not about working harder; but it does involve living by a philosophy of under-promising and over-delivering. Even if you promise to move heaven and earth make sure you deliver the universe, metaphorically speaking. The key is of course to love what you do because people don't die from hard work; they die from hard work they don't like. If you can't go the extra mile you're in the wrong role.

Motivating Ambassadorial Alliances

When you do take that extra mile it sends a very clear signal to others as to how much you value them. When people know that you genuinely value them they become ambassadors to your cause.

The responsibility of entrepreneurial leaders and managers is to educate every one of their people in the importance of putting emotional value into what they do. They can do this by treating their people in the same way as their best clients, because they in turn are the businesses front-line to the customers.

This develops a customer ethos conducive to loyalty. Customers no longer tolerate being treated as another transaction or a statistic on a survey sheet. Trust, of course, is the very foundation of any lasting relationship. When you are building trust it is vital that you deliver what you promise to others, whether they be friends or customers. Why treat a customer any different to a colleague or friend? Why charge customers for additional service that you wouldn't charge a friend?

Imagine, for example, you buy a car, and late one night you break your key off in the lock. One call to a Sewell Cadillac garage, the US's leading luxury car dealer and their twenty-four hour service will come and fix it for you, without charging. They may charge for something slightly more serious, but their whole customer ethos is based on providing the same kind of service for customers as they would for a good friend.

Founder Carl Sewell's passion is turning one-time buyers into lifetime customers, treating his colleagues like customers and in turn they all become ambassadors for Sewell Cadillacs in return. Sewell's philosophy is keeping customers for life by offering free, friendly service for certain peace of mind jobs makes better sense than paying huge advertising sums to build an image that may attract customers.

The only source of competitive advantage a business has is its people and the service they provide. Good customer service that builds loyalty is too important to be passed to some customer relations department, so people must be copowered to resolve problems. Everybody must be a customer service ambassador for his or her company because that is how the customer perceives it to be anyway.

Like any good ambassador people must be absolutely sure about what they do and why they do it. They are the catalysts for turning every one of their one-time customers that choose to buy from them into lifetime customers. It is the little things that count in service, never the big things and people become ambassadors aligned to your business when such thoughtfulness exists.

Imagine again, for example, purchasing something and then finding when you got home that it was faulty. You would not be very happy, particularly if you had made a special trip into town to buy it. Upon contacting the business, however, imagine how you would feel if the person who sold you the item called you right back, apologised for your inconvenience and promised to arrange for another to be delivered to your home that very day. Then phoned you in the evening to make sure you received it!

Now, that may cost the business more than the product value, but it would be a considerably smaller amount than the amount required in advertising costs required to build a good image to improve customer relations. Because an immediate solution to the problem had been provided, your loyalty to that business would begin to grow. The value of a loyal customer who is more than happy to be an *ambassador* for a business is immeasurable.

> **Competitive advantage is a business's people and the service they provide.**

Every front-line person at Disney, even if they are short-term, who has first contact with the customer, undergoes regular training on customer service. Car park attendants, for example, have six weeks training because he or she is such an important ambassador.

Often a business that wants long-term growth will hope for better service and greater loyalty, but have a reward system that is linked to sale quantity. Strategy might well be focused on the long-term profits, but as bonuses are often paid only on the short-term, employees focus on short-term budgets instead of long-term growth. The point is that whatever is rewarded gets done. Business will not get from its people what it may hope for. Business will only get from them what it rewards.

A business may hire employees and managers to serve customers face to face, but then 'reward' them with a low flat hourly wage and provide little or no training in the basics of how to provide good service. The reward, therefore, may as well be interpreted as simply minding the shop. As for those people that are employed in support of the customer but have no actual contact with them, any customer linked reward or recognition for effort is non-existent.

It seems ridiculous that so many businesses give so little training and pay to the front-line positions, yet expect them to give excellent service. Then when the complaints flood in, the cry is: 'you can't get good people these days.' Peter Drucker's question to a group of CEO's when they were admitting to him that all of their people were not up to much encapsulates such thinking: 'Were they like that when you hired them, or did you make them that way?'

A customer-focused-ethos compny must view both its people and customers as ambassadors rewarding them for delivering excellent service and for being customers respectively. The consequences that a customer or potential customer will experience from their action through contacting a business, or one of its ambassadors, will influence future behaviour. When rewarded for their custom they continue it and become ambassadors. The alternative is that they will become someone else's customer and be motivated to be a competitor's emissary.

Both people and customers alike must become allies in recommending because people buy from word of mouth. In an early chapter of the first Harry Potter book, The Philosophers Stone, I read: 'the world will know about Harry Potter.'

The publishing phenomenon that followed happened simply because everyone who read it became an ambassador for it – because they enjoyed it. And most importantly, they had already become future ambassadors for all the books in the series. Life-time customers were created because the initial product offering delivered its promise and the first people who picked it up became advocates and ambassadors.

By way of another example, say you open a new restaurant. Everyone is excited but very nervous about whether everything will be all right. Everyone working there wants to make everything work out well because they also have bills and other living expenses to pay. When the doors first open, therefore, everyone rewards customers for booking and arriving with highly attentive service, thoughtful behaviour and a friendly welcoming attitude. Within a few months your business is performing really well, with customers returning again and again and new ones pouring in. Your people and your customers are ambassadors for the business.

Inevitably you start to feel confident because there is so much business to handle and though you may have been a bit abrupt with that last customer, you don't concern yourself too much because there are plenty more coming through the door. But it's at this point that the paradox of success begins to materialise.

In the ensuing months you are the last to realise that the attention to customers, the quality of service and the intention to perform as well as possible has insidiously declined. With fewer customers and falling sales you keep behind the scenes, busily devising cost cutting plans, special offers and writing copy for some advertising that someone has suggested you really ought to do.

You layoff a couple of former staff who had become *ambassadors*, you reduce the portions of the meals, rationalising that they were far too generous before, but still the customers, previously good ambassadors for your business, don't come back. You blame the economy, the weather and the new competition that has just opened so that you feel that it's not your fault. The fact remains that it is.

You stopped rewarding the customers and they voted with their feet. In the beginning you made them feel so special, and they liked it and supported your business by coming back again and telling their friends. Then, when business boomed, you began to take them for granted and they withdrew their support.

Some even felt cheated. It's that simple. Now, perhaps if you had rewarded your ambassadors nothing would have changed and the business would have continued to grow. When your focus changed you unwittingly stopped driving the business, but continued running it into the ground. Your ambassadors simply followed your example.

With our inherent craving for meaning and purpose, whenever we receive praise for our efforts or rewards for achieving our goals, we feel appreciated, valued and meaningful. Therefore, good business management always starts with clearly communicated expectations, as to the kind of behaviour and results they want. Entrepreneurial corporations look upon everyone as an opportunity to develop an ambassadorial alliance. They do so through right treatment and training and genuinely valuing and rewarding them.

Building Champion Synergy

Not *every* salesperson may be an ambassador, but every ambassador must be a customer-focused salesperson because, regardless of role they represent their company. Those who are employed behind the scenes may not always understand how they can be salespeople until it is pointed out to them.

Of the four hundred people involved in the London Churchill Hotel that made up housekeeping, engineering, security, reception and operating employees, banqueting and restaurant, there were just five salespeople.

In establishing the desired results, the measured goals and the reward and recognition programme, it was suggested that every one of the four hundred employees should be an ambassador for their hotel by talking about the benefits it offered to whosoever asked. Giving a person a sense of pride in what they do, by giving them a piece of the action with a reward, is a tremendous motivator and energy builder.

The proposal was that everyone 'sells' *one* room per year, without pressure, through word of mouth using their own network. What was asked seemed reasonable and attainable, so everyone bought into it. They became ambassadors, with some departments even working together in teams agreeing to pool efforts. All four hundred ambassadors achieved at least a single occupancy as suggested.

They all enjoyed success and the benefits of both reward and recognition. As for the service, it became outstanding because, with 'ambassadors' guests regularly staying, everyone strove to be the best they could possibly be. Every single employee became a committed ambassador knowing that their reward is for doing what they are good at, which is looking after the customer.

Everyone wants to be part of a winning team. Give people a piece of the action and they'll think *customer*. Give them work they love to do and reward them well for doing it and they'll think *customer*. Build in promotion and increased responsibilities, but with the freedom to steer their own goals toward fulfilment, and they'll think *customer*. Give them incentives in the form of prizes, whether tickets to the theatre and sport events, dinners or even holidays and they'll think *customer*.

It takes financial courage to treat people in such a way that they accept, without question, that the customer must always come first. Entrepreneurial organisations understand that rewarding the customer is *everyone's* responsibility and rewarding those who look after the customer is the responsibility of leadership. But it takes courage to operate your business by always putting customers first and to invest in developing entrepreneurial service.

Businesses that employ ambassadors to work with them, not for them, to fulfil a common purpose, with shared values and common objectives will ultimately be the highly profitable ones. When such ambassadors choose to align what they do, with what they are, taking ownership of fulfilling their own personal mission is facilitated. A mission that recognises that the best way to serve your self is through good service to others.

> **Ambassadorial alliances are relationships founded on recommendation and reassurance.**

Synergy is about people working together, generating an enthusiastic energy that causes others to buy into what they are involved in. Making people very much a part of what they do develops them into championing what they do. Such champion synergy is a fundamental element of ambassadorial alliances, which go beyond strategic alliances.

Strategic alliances allow an company to gain muscle without necessarily getting heavily weighed down; provide research and development advantages; cost efficiency and greater value chains. Yet ambassadorial alliances allow people, customers and network relationships to enjoy a virtuous circle of growth and success through recommendation and reassurance. Think of all the factors that influence and affect your life on a day-to-day basis. It is recommendation-driven either by someone or by your own to another. Now imagine how your own company would grow with such entrepreneurial endorsement.

Duplicating and Following Through

Over two thirds of customers are lost to business because of apathy. The opposite of apathy is following through. Entrepreneurially-minded corporations are able to maximize on opportunity because most business do not follow through. Yet, it is at the traditional close of the sale that the entrepreneurial start begins.

Entrepreneurial leader L. Dennis Kozlowski's business philosophy is to duplicate and follow through, *always* follow through. Having acquired 120 organisations in under ten years increasing turnover from $3b revenue to over $30Bn with low staff turnover he has led Tyco International Inc. into a multi-billion conglomerate worth more than Ford and General Motors combined.

In true entrepreneurial organisational style he shuns memos, staff meetings, and bureaucracy yet with just 140 corporate colleagues at a modest two storey headquarters handles a corporation of over 200,000 people. Voted one of the top ten best CEO's in the US, twice, he believes that most business opportunities fail because they are not followed through effectively and that the wrong people are in the wrong role. Those people then fail to duplicate what works.

It is not the structure that is at fault, it is the service of following through what you have started. In Tyco's entrepreneurial culture managers are copowered with enormous autonomy. In acquiring another company, which Tyco does almost on a monthly basis, Kozlowski believes that the best way to maintain synergy and follow through is to promote a new boss from among its current staff. 'Then they feel they're part of our team and contributing to a new start.' He believes that one of the big reasons mergers fail is management problems. Although companies often spend many hours and many millions poring over the financials and the strategic fit, they pay little attention to crucial personnel issues until it's far too late.

Kozlowski spends most of his time on the road so he can meet and visit with employees, investors, and customers. He squeezes the most out of these operations with ultra-lean and decentralized management. Kozlowski hates meetings with a passion, preferring to keep in touch by PC and phone. Any detailed information that is required is always available because he trusts his team to perform. To duplicate he seeks out managers that are cast in the same mold as himself.

For an entrepreneurial culture to work everyone must think entrepreneurially. Motivation is based on a demanding compensation plan that delivers a bonus equal to salary when targets are hit. But if they go beyond the target, the sky's the limit. One of his team, Jurgen W. Gromer received a base salary of £625,000, yet because he exceeded the target by 300% his bonus was $13m. Kozlowski's personal goal is to leave behind a corporation that's considered one of the best in the world. Putting his money where his mouth is, all of his Tyco stock remains in the organisation. Others follow his lead.

When entrepreneurial leaders duplicate themselves successfully, they set themselves free while generating greater success for their company. The measure of successful duplication is quite simple; are all the stakeholders benefiting from added value. To be a master of duplication is to copower through trust and delegation. The mastery begins when you know your own strengths that generate value, and are able to bring out the strengths of others to do the same. It is hard to find others that will be in your mold but the key is to be guided by the chemistry over and above the career resume; and then put them in a position to develop through hands-on experience, in a sponsored business unit initiative.

Look for people with track records that have already done the things that you want to duplicate. Do not look for extraordinary people. Look for ordinary people and train them for extraordinary things. Always look first within your own organisation because they will already share vision and values and hopefully understand what you do about your business. They may even know more. Look for people that have the courage to make and take decisions and will work harder than what they are paid for and choose innovative ways to serve profitably beyond the brief. Above all, look for people that are opportunity-focused and know how to create value.

Effectively you are duplicating yourself, so when you act in the manner of an entrepreneurial leader you will discover that synchronicity will actually work in your favour, you will attract the right people to you because they will be motivated to follow your lead. In this way, you are sure that your company will comprise of giants and not dwarfs.

People buy people and with such people, treated right your business will attract both quantity and quality customers that in turn act as ambassadors. With such internal and external ambassadorial networking comes greater opportunity.

> **To be a master of duplication is to copower through trust and delegation.**

Chapter 7
Creating Entrepreneurial Opportunities

OPPORTUNITY, IN THE WORLD OF BUSINESS, is *always* right in front of our faces. The crime is that for most of our time we are either too preoccupied to be aware of it, or just not interested in looking for it. Even if we do see it then either we don't recognise it because we are uncertain about what we are looking for, or are just too busy, or lethargic, to do anything about it. The whole point about entrepreneurship is about seeking *new* opportunity, capturing it and creating value out of it. When we do select whatever it is we are looking for and proactively pursue it we often discover that opportunities relating to it actually find us. The very act of being on the look out for opportunity *creates* opportunity.

Creating both an entrepreneurial people culture and customer ethos ensures that all stakeholders involved from creating to maximising opportunity enjoy significant beneficial value. The fact is that entrepreneurial corporations that become good at it are inundated with opportunity. The Matsushita Corporation generated over a staggering 6m ideas within its organisation in the last year. With each member proposing an idea every week on average it is evident that its entrepreneurial culture of putting people before products and service before structure is highly successful.

With such a magnitude of ideas it is clear that there is a successful communication, process and reward system in place. Otherwise, there would be no motivation for such an idea avalanche. Matsushita is actually more an innovator to bring products to market than an inventor of products to market. So not surprisingly they are very successful at serving customers. With everyone involved in a company acting as entrepreneurial ambassadors endorsing their products through their own networks and receiving ideas in feedback they have a culture of creating opportunity and enjoying it. Such a 'fun factor' is very often spoken about as essential to organisational culture, yet in reality is hard to attain. People that are ambassadors for what they do enjoy themselves more than people that are not. When commitment is lacking, even though they may be well rewarded and recognised for what they do, people will not be motivated to be creative nor deliver up their creativity.

> **Opportunity is always right in front us.**
> **Our crime is being too preoccupied to be**
> **aware of it, or just uninterested in looking.**

Consignia which incorporates the Royal Mail, a 350-year-old UK based business, has a similar number of 'employees' as Matsushita has 'ambassadors.' Yet ideas generated by its people are just a tiny fraction. Getting ideas through the current thirteen layers of hierarchy is frustrating and time-consuming with no defined recognition or reward even if successful. Many of the ideas that create opportunity naturally come from customers.

Consignia, with its monopoly of delivering mail however, has a culture that still considers it is doing the 'general public' a favour. Consequently, there is a lack of inclination to listen to customer needs. For example: despite the enormous success of its US counterpart's initiative to *receive* mail from its customer's homes the need has still not been recognised, let alone anticipated, in the UK. In fairness, state owned Consignia have recognised that such a strategic change is essential for their future, and are genuinely working to move towards a more entrepreneurial culture. Currently, they are in the process of determining the most appropriate methodology to do so.

History has always proved that the greater the obstacle the greater the opportunity that will be forthcoming because of the obstacle. The 350-year-old heritage currently vested in Consignia has already overcome many obstacles but ultimately has been protected by a monopolistic advantage that is no longer a realistic protection. Overcoming what is now clearly its greatest obstacle to date of learning how to become a 21st century organisation that fully utilises the potential of its established network, experience and knowledge, will create massive opportunity for it. The danger is that time may run out for it and more entrepreneurially-minded competitors take away its core competency.

Ideas that create opportunity are of course worthless by themselves, irrespective of how good they are. Only ideas implemented and followed through have any chance of creating value. So, unless there is a system for distilling the ideas from generation through to evaluation and on to testing, implementation and market success, having ideas will be purely academic.

What is important is to never stop the process of reviewing how products and services are taken to the market; to persistently cultivate innovative ways of doing things differently and seek out gaps and niches in the market that create opportunity; and to build, and actively utilise to the full, an essential network that provides the never-ending supply of valuable ideas that maintains entrepreneurial purpose.

Reviewing how we go to Market

'I liked it so much, I bought the company,' said Victor Kiam. With entrepreneurial spirit and management skills, this Harvard graduate met both his biggest obstacle and greatest opportunity when he bought Remington, a company that had no future according to the analysts. The way that he took the product to market turned the fortunes of the company around. His delight as a customer spawned his belief in the product and stimulated his thinking because 'Since I liked it other men with faces would'. To me his market strategy illustrated the importance of having a customer first and a business plan second.

Most organisations will prepare detailed business plans relating to how a new product or service will succeed in an established market. As entrepreneurship is about creating new opportunities it is important to be aware of establishing markets and emerging trends or gaps within a well-established market. I believe that any new idea must first be matched with a customer even before a business plan is considered. Often, when asked to comment on business plans, I have to admit that the presentation and thought they comprise is frequently so outstanding that many finance sources may be persuaded to provide immediate support. My first comment even before reading them, however, is in the form of a question: Do you have a customer?

Of course, how a plan is presented is vitally important in gaining support for an idea. But the simple napkin doodle, motivated by the reason that there is a customer, is more effective than the brilliantly prepared business plan that does not yet have a customer. The argument is that it is not always possible to simply identify a customer. They may not know what they want until they see it. My response to this argument is to present a simple test. As the question: 'Would you be a customer for what you are presenting? For if it doesn't interest you, then how is it possible to inject the passion, so essential to entrepreneurship, to enthuse others?

The best way to go to market is to seek out those gaps that you recognise as annoyingly unfulfilled, similar to those entrepreneurial-minded customers that asked: 'Why can't they make vacuum cleaners without the bag?' 'Why can't there be a clockwork radio? 'Why can't there be a pocket communicator?' 'Why is that not convenient?' 'Why don't they do this?' 'If we have a distribution channel do we use it effectively?'

In the early 1980's a colleague started a wine importation business simply by utilising lorries that used to return empty after delivering produce to Europe. The timing took advantage of the emerging trend towards wine drinking in the UK and the company went on to supply a national supermarket. It was also an early template soon mimicked for using distribution chains both ways and thus more effectively. The mail division of Consignia has a massive distribution chain able to reach 22 million homes in the UK. From a customer's perspective, however, it is currently utilised as a one-way street to deliver junk mail.

An corporation must regularly review how it goes to market and ask why it does in the way that it does, because established organisations can unwittingly develop a habit of swiftly getting out of touch with their market. The classic example of this is how the powerful Decca Records, later to disappear, turned down the opportunity to sign up the Beatles, because they believed guitar music in groups was no longer marketable.

A more recent publishing equivalent example is how companies turned down the Harry Potter books, a 21st century phenomenon; because they believed that the style was not marketable. Both illustrate the dangers of becoming cocooned from the market that sustains you. What has always fascinated me is the way business spends fortunes on developing a product without literally 'walking the streets' of its market first. It then goes on to spend further fortunes in marketing to justify a product's development.

If value is created from an opportunity because the people at street level are inspired by it, then it makes good sense to 'walk the streets' for inspiration. In walking the streets for hours at a time,

Charles Dickens received his inspiration to write and also, importantly, gained his sensitive understanding of what his readers would be interested in. His book *A Christmas Carol* was the catalyst for 'inventing' the celebratory form of Christmas we now know and which is arguably the most successful time for retailers.

> **As understanding what inspires people at street-level leads to creating value from opportunity, it makes good sense to 'walk the streets' for inspiration.**

It was Coca Cola at the turn of the 20th century that gave Santa Claus his red suit. No one today, however, associates Christmas with Coca Cola because the organisation regularly reviews its market place.

The way politicians seeking election understand their market place is by getting out into the street and talking to the masses. Unfortunately, and not dissimilar to corporations, too often they lose touch with their electorate customers, forgetting that their position has been gained because of them. Reviewing the market means revisiting it to see first hand if there are changes that demand adapting to.

Most market opportunities actually already exist but are simply overlooked. In reviewing how we go to market we discover these opportunities. Entrepreneurial organisations must ask questions along the lines of the following:

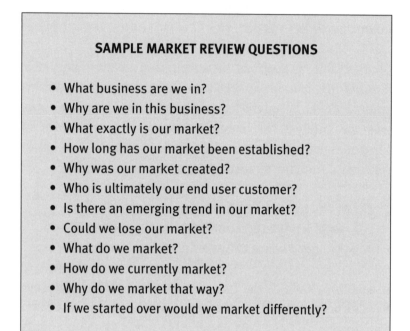

SAMPLE MARKET REVIEW QUESTIONS

- What business are we in?
- Why are we in this business?
- What exactly is our market?
- How long has our market been established?
- Why was our market created?
- Who is ultimately our end user customer?
- Is there an emerging trend in our market?
- Could we lose our market?
- What do we market?
- How do we currently market?
- Why do we market that way?
- If we started over would we market differently?

Applying The One-Percent Solution (T.O.P.S.)

Revisiting the market to remind us of our understanding of it and getting in touch with what we think we know and need to know, is an integral part of creating opportunity. Cultivating both innovation and opportunity spotting must be done all the time and throughout the entire entrepreneurial organisation.

The most effective way to introduce this is to use the power of The One-Percent Solution. In *Born to Succeed*, I recommended that if just 14 minutes of each day were engaged in personal evaluation, the other 99 % of our life would greatly benefit. Treating yourself as 'You inc.' or 'You plc' in other words boss of your own corporation where you are the CEO with a lifetime contract, is a powerful methodology for releasing potential. Over the years I have developed the concept further and discovered that when applied to creating an entrepreneurial organisation the methodology proved highly beneficial in generating ideas and solutions that cultivate innovation and create opportunity.

The hardest part of any culture change is growing *continuously* the new habits required. Good programs that prove very fertile sow seeds that sprout only to whither shortly afterwards, starved of daily action. Good habits, whether entrepreneurial or whatever, do not happen overnight. But for them to become firmly established and thus provide beneficial value they must be developed on a *daily* basis.

Revisiting the basics, I remember as a child impatiently having to wait 21-day periods for laid eggs to hatch. Watching an inert object suddenly change into a new life was always worth the wait. Transformation came about because of daily attendance by the mother hen. Few will argue that if you can stick at something on a daily basis for at least three weeks there is a good chance that you will benefit from what seems to suddenly become a new habit. The secret is not to spend too much time consciously thinking about something, but to do so on a daily basis. Though our greater subconscious is always working either for or against us, depending on our thoughts, when it is reminded daily about something that we want to know, or need to find, it stays on track and delivers for us.

Asking for less than 15 minutes of your own or someone else's time is reasonable, particularly when it is for a positive purpose. With 1,440 minutes in everyone's day spending just 1% of it either to solve a problem or generate an idea makes good sense and works with significant results. Its acceptance and application is made simple for many individuals because it does not even impinge on their day. People will either rise earlier or retire later each day, depending on their preference, by the required 14 minutes. Indeed, having a 14-minute appointment to concentrate on something meaningful to you galvanises your thoughts that often lack purpose.

When the One-Percent Solution [T.O.P.S.] is applied within a team, company or organisation, the effects are multiplied exponentially. With everyone working on a particular solution the power of a collective consciousness is invoked. From an entrepreneurial perspective, this is almost like receiving manna from heaven. Why? Because one of the most important habitual skills of entrepreneurship is to *anticipate* wants, recognise *establishing* markets, understand *emerging* trends and create opportunity.

Team application of The One-Percent Solution is significant; applying it to an organisation has an exponential effect.

Often when one person has an idea, another somewhere is having the same. But it will be the entrepreneurial-minded person that takes action. Similarly when one company has a market-boosting concept another company somewhere is having the same. However, only the entrepreneurial organisation will take the appropriate action. The non-action takers have to admit in frustration to having had the same idea when they later learn that the concept has been implemented with success. When an organisation is able to develop the habit of internally growing the ideas and solutions it starts on the path to consistently cultivating innovation and creating great opportunities.

Applying The One-Percent Solution on a team basis requires choosing just one question at first to build the habit; and agreeing that all members will mark in their diaries a daily 14-minute convenient appointment with themselves to actively address the question. The time period should be no more and no less. When proven methodology for getting fit is ignored those people eager to get fit quickly overdo it and suffer injury. Making an appointment is important because it ensures that application of The One-Percent Solution is taken seriously. Usually the level of question dispels scepticism. If, for example, when seeking an answer to the question: *'Is there an emerging trend in our market?'* it leads to identifying an opportunity that can alter an organisation's share price, why should T.O.P.S. not be taken seriously?

Entrepreneurs instrumental in founding successful and established corporations have always applied such methods of relaxed-intensity for inspiration. The point is, when you apply regular conscious effort your subconscious, and the collective conscious of your colleagues, actually generates a gravitation towards seeing the solution or opportunity, even if it was right in front of you all along.

The principle behind the concept is simple; when we know what we are looking for, we will recognise signals that lead to finding it. All of us regularly experience seeing a new word only to come across it again several times within a short time. All of us experience seeing the evidence of something that we have been previously thinking about such as, how a particular model and color of a car appears everywhere after we have thought about getting one.

The practice itself is common sense because it involves taking the time to do something that works. Most people are too busy to think; too busy earning money to make money; too busy getting out of what they don't want to do, than getting on with what they want to do.

Many of the questions that have been asked throughout this book will provide valuable answers applying T.O.P.S. Project teams within business unit initiatives will gain valuable insight by applying, in a more scientific way, what is already expected of members. Email facilitates the communication of the question requiring a solution. In any business of course and in any team meeting, whenever a solution is being sought, everyone is expected to 'think about it' ready for discussion at the next meeting. But the reality is that although they may have the intention to, most people do not take the time to 'think about it' because there are always too many other things to think about. Consequently, 'thinking about it' is habitually applied 'just in time' before the next meeting. Seldom is it applied on a daily basis.

Certainly the most effective way to develop The One-Percent Solution is actively to practice it. In applying T.O.P.S. over the next 21 days for example within your own team, and of course independently, you will discover significant results. In addition, you will strengthen your self-discipline and, importantly, your skill for creating opportunity. Furthermore, you will be moving your organisation towards establishing a creative culture, that sought after climate so conducive for entrepreneurial organisations. When everyone is given the opportunity to be involved in delivering solutions that will impact the whole organisation, the business-owner paradigm is also strengthened.

Full-time attention to creating either an entrepreneurially-minded culture or cultivating innovation and opportunity is not possible, particularly in an established organisation. Part-time attention on any culture change will not work. Daily attention, as required by T.O.P.S., is possible and *does* work. It is *always* the little things that make the biggest difference, turning around failure into success. The One-Percent Solution makes the difference that creates added value for 99% of organisational success.

> **Developing the habit of internally growing the ideas and solutions an organisation consistently cultivates innovation and creates opportunities.**

Building an Entrepreneurial Network

It's not what you know and it's not who you know. It's what you do with what you know with who you know. Networks and networking have always been the foundation stones for business building and never more so than now. Living in the age of the knowledge-worker operating within excellence-driven and relationship-driven business models such stones are vital for success. The end of the Stone Age of course did not come about because of lack of stones. Similarly, the knowledge-worker will not disappear because of lack of knowledge. But what they have to offer will be purely academic unless there is proactive harnessing and effective utilisation of networking in order to ensure that such knowledge is practicably applied to create value.

With the abundance of databases, coupled with the practical advantages the Internet provides, gaining access to both contacts and knowledge has never been easier. When, at the touch of a finger, selected and detailed knowledge can be both sent and received it is not surprising that agile entrepreneurial business initiatives are thriving. The speed and ease of moving information assists in maintaining communication and helping to build a network of resources. But it is not sufficient to rely on technology to build a network because entrepreneurial networks are founded on relationships. The reason why entrepreneurs build networks, through primary and secondary social and business networking, is to overcome obstacles, open doors and access resources.

In the early 1990's requiring 'additional' income, to weather the recession at the time, I learned of Network Marketing, a form of home shopping through recommendation that utilised personal networks. Within the short period of 12 months from becoming involved as an independent distributor with Fortune 500 Company, National Safety Associates, I had built an international network of 3,000 people. Such a network had grown from a small percentage of the personal contact list, which I had been recommended to prepare, that comprised 100 names. Turnover reached $1m dollars generating a net income of $1,000 a week, and I received shares in the company in recognition of the achievement before selling my distributorship. Sharing the concept as a business opportunity is not the purpose of the example. My point is to illustrate the power of networking because such a strategy is important for entrepreneurial corporations.

Networking is a low-cost, 'getting – in – touch – with – the – street methodology for learning about the marketplace and gathering information and further contacts. It involves talking to people, making contacts, keeping in touch and following through when appropriate for mutual benefit. There are two types of relationship in networking: Firm and Fair, which range from close friends and family to regular acquaintances and friendly colleagues; and Contacts, which comprise all other forms of other social interaction.

Everyone knows at least 100 people, whether Firm and Fair or Contacts. So, in seeking, creating or selecting an opportunity to pursue, it makes good sense to select those people that you already know, and believe will be willing to either provide insightful information or appropriate contacts to assist your efforts. This is where established non-entrepreneurial organisations do not utilise their people potential to the full. Conversely, ambassadors of the entrepreneurial organisation can be willingly encouraged to share information and contacts when involved in pursuing an opportunity.

Opportunity ideas come from three main areas: insight into emerging trends, either through market data or reflection;

inspiration that leads to something new or innovative; and from talking to people. The individual entrepreneur views all interaction with others, whether accidental, unplanned, planned, long-term, short-term or fleeting as an opportunity to construct a network of his or her business resources. Indeed, they will either have a contact for whatever is currently wanted, or, and this is important, have no concern in immediately making contact with whomsoever they learn is the right source.

An established organisation, of course, usually has a detailed database of contacts. Indeed, it is accepted that such a database is vital. My own experience of many organisations, however, is that their database is utterly under-utilised and seldom kept up to date. Entrepreneurial leaders, therefore, must first ensure that there is a relevant database, reviewed regularly and applied appropriately for selected initiatives.

Secondly they must encourage colleagues and teams to develop contact lists. Such a process is in the spirit of supporting service before structure. The purpose of the contacts list is to serve as a reminder to the individual as to the contacts that they do have, but have forgotten about. Their purpose is not to be posted for the benefit of all, but they can remind the individual of the mutual benefit of having contacts.

Whenever you meet someone, irrespective of the circumstances, there is almost always 'common ground' discovered in the form of knowing the same people. The common refrain of 'It's a small world' often leads to learning about something of interest and value and forming a relationship that provides a future win:win situation for the parties involved. This is not often the case because for most of the time people do not actually network, even though they may be exposed to a networking opportunity.

I am always surprised at how people at functions choose to remain in their internal groups gossiping, rather than network in external groups with people that are often experts in alternative industries with valuable ideas and opportunities to share. Such input of diversity will always provide added value for entrepreneurial-minded individuals, as it provides knowledge of potential markets, location of alternative resources, innovations and of course opportunity-in-waiting.

Everyone has valuable contacts. For your own valuable resource I would recommend that you take the time to write a list of 100 contacts. The very action of this exercise will stimulate your thinking into 'seeing' an opportunity that you have previously ignored or overlooked. The point of the exercise is that upon experiencing the results yourself you will see the enormous value of consistently and persistently building a network for creating and following through opportunity.

Groups of decentralised units whether the 4,000 in 3M or the 200 autonomous companies under the Virgin brand network with each other for resources. And remember, it is the individuals within organisations that make things happen because of their contact-knowledge. Too many organisations have units that keep things to themselves worry that sister units will 'steal' ideas. Lack of liaison within an corporation is a major reason for it to literally miss out on opportunity. When the strength of all resources is brought together there is greater success. Once you do make contacts, maintain them. They are an entrepreneurial resource.

Maintaining Entrepreneurial Purpose

Moving towards being an entrepreneurial organisation is one thing, maintaining an entrepreneurial purpose is another. People make up organisations and they can insidiously become comfortable, complacent or cocoon themselves from their markets and customers because they are so busy either being successful or important. Such common action makes you mistake propaganda for purpose.

The president of a global corporation told me how easy it was to start thinking that you were some kind of demi-god when, during the good times, every one of your 100,000 people was intent on telling you what a good job you were doing. Such invulnerability vanishes when times change and the huge TV screens you have in your office that once displayed soaring growth then report the opposite. Losing sight of your purpose and believing instead your own propaganda inevitably leads to receiving a jolt that: 'leaves your ego teetering on the edge of a self-built precipice realising that you were mortal after all.'

Transforming the US energy group, Enron, from staid utility to high-energy entrepreneurial performer illustrates at first the immense value of blending good management with entrepreneurial spirit. Within 10 years of reducing numerous hierarchal levels to a flatter structure and minimising bureaucracy; and creating an atmosphere that was rewarded for thinking out-of-the-box, the company went from zero to hero gaining a position within the top 10 of the Fortune 500 ahead of IBM and Bank of America.

The approach of the entrepreneurial leader, Jeffrey Skilling, tasked with moving Enron towards entrepreneurship was to correctly stimulate innovation and entrepreneurial thinking for growth. So long as you clear your ideas through the tight central control of risk, legal, finance, performance evaluation and remuneration 'People could do whatever you want around here.' But the balance of maintaining an organisation that harnesses both entrepreneurial characteristics and good management must not be allowed to tip too far one way or the other.

Enron swung too much to that form that distinguishes the start-up entrepreneur that lacks management skills, from the professionally managed entrepreneurial corporation. Over zealous executives began to over-promise and under-deliver on new ventures and Enron's credibility suffered, culminating in the biggest corporate failure in history. Enron's successful growth was due to entrepreneurial thinking; its demise was due to neither cultivating the basics nor adhering to good management. The whole point of developing entrepreneurial attributes within an corporation is to ensure that the application of proven management and leadership skills are the most effective they can possibly be.

The collapse of it's business quickly followed. A learning curve is of course good for creating the established entrepreneurial organisation. What is important is that organisations do revisit the basics and apply the principles and practices of entrepreneurial leadership to stay both in balance and on track. Entrepreneurial purpose must be continuously maintained of course otherwise organisations will quickly revert to bureaucratic control structures instead of more profitable service-focused places of learning and enjoyment. Furthermore, the economies of scope for maintaining such purpose are reflected in reputation for being entrepreneurial. With such a reputation ideas and opportunities are constantly knocking at your door because success breeds success.

The new entrepreneurial-minded corporation will sustain itself more effectively than the non-entrepreneurial-minded one because it will create *and attract* a continuous source of innovation; the key ingredient for economic prosperity. It will also retain *and recruit* the right people for the right role with entrepreneurial spirit; the key ingredient for maintaining entrepreneurial purpose and leading the challenge.

> **Maintaining entrepreneurial purpose ensures corporations remain profitable service-focussed places of learning and enjoyment, preventing reversion to bureaucratic control structures.**

Leading the Challenge

Another energy company, Royal Dutch Shell, are committed to contribute to sustainable development; offer customers new products and services; creating an extensive portfolio of opportunities; and meeting society's expectations for long-term success. To do so they have recognised the challenge to move towards creating entrepreneurial-minded behaviour. This adheres to the conviction that innovative organisations will always be successful particularly when they are able release the entrepreneurial potential of their people.

One president of Royal Dutch Shell, Jeroen van de Veer initiated a methodology entitled GameChanger to capture and drive through innovations guided by entrepreneurial management. New ideas for projects that are generated receive an evaluated response within a 30-day period, which is both an incentive to generate ideas and accelerates the actionable process of them. There is an agreed budget and initiatives are supported, and networked, to ensure cross-fertilization of ideas and common access to innovation, contacts and tools.

The GameChanger mechanism in their exploration and production, for example, leads to regular initiatives being set up in Shell ventures, some evolving to multi-million dollar businesses. The entrepreneurial individuals that proposed and drove the project receive stock, or when sold as some are, become part of the new company and stockholders. Govert Boeles, of Shell told me that the methodology stands-out because: 'we allow experiments and reward testing propositions on a small scale, even if they fail.'

The challenges for organisations include reducing hierarchy to flatter more decisive and agile structures that are able to swiftly respond to emerging markets and anticipate customer wants. In creating mini-enterprises within such structure they will have the benefit of a strong integrated interdependent nature that shares resources as appropriate because of its network mindset.

Such a challenge may sound like swimming upstream. To use a metaphorical example, only live salmon can swim upstream and only strong ones overcome all obstacles; in doing so new life is once again created. Old salmon die but only after having spawned literally thousands of new eggs. Established corporations will have to come to terms with the fact that they must behave differently. The reward for successfully doing so is that hundreds of profitable business units will be created from within its nucleus. These units with their entrepreneurial-behaviour and skilled management will ensure that the new, more entrepreneurial-minded, organisation is able to fulfil its purpose of realising its potential.

Creating corporate entrepreneurship demands acknowledging at individual, team and strategic level the importance of lifelong learning. Established organisations that seek a quick-fix program to introduce entrepreneurial behaviour because years of bureaucratic control that have stymied innovation are seriously reducing returns will be disappointed unless there is commitment to a never-ending education and application of entrepreneurship.

Learning and living entrepreneurial principles builds character; and once implemented the practices improve excellence. Such principles and practices must not be viewed as a 'to do' list to mark off when mastered because the entrepreneurial leadership success they deliver requires consistency and persistency. The nature of developing entrepreneurial leadership involves trust, courage and forgiveness. Developing confidence in such vital virtues that allow people to think as business owners, feel copowered and act as ambassadors takes time. The very daily process of such thinking, behaviour and action, however, is the stimulus that will drive organisations to *continuously* fulfil their potential and realise the purpose for which they were founded.

Reaping Success

Recreating the characteristics of entrepreneurship and developing entrepreneurial leadership throughout will revitalise the corporation originally founded by the very same characteristics and leadership. It is not so much about reinventing as rediscovering, redefining and re-implementing such attributes that repeatedly ensure future success. Harnessing and re-instilling the spirit of entrepreneurship with skilled management is the most effective way to reassure all stakeholders, re-energize leaders and receive the reward of success.

Further Reading

Bailey, Andrew and Egan, Gerard, *Talkworks: How To Get More Out Of Life Through Better Communications* British Telecommunications plc 1999).

Bennis, Warren, Speitzer, Gretchen M. and Cummings, Thomas G. (editors), *The Future of Leadership* (Jossey-Bass Publishers 2001).

Bidault, Francis, Depres, Charles and Butler, Christina, *Leveraged Innovation* (Macmillan Press Ltd. 1998).

Birley, Sue and Muzyka, Daniel F., *Mastering Entrepreneurship* (*Financial Times* Prentice Hall 2000).

Collins, James C. and Porras, Jerry I., *Built to Last: Successful Habits of Visionary Companies* (Random House Business Books 2000).

Davis, Steven I., *Leadership in Conflict: The Lessons of History* (Macmillan Press Ltd. 1996).

Day, Laura, *Practical Intuition: How to Harness the Power of Instinct and Make it work for You* (Vermillion 1997).

Essex, Louellen and Kusy, Mitchell, *Fast Forward Leadership (Financial Times* Prentice hall 1999).

Freemantle, David, *What Customers Like About You* (Nicolas Brealey Publishing 1998).

Goltz, Jay, *The Street-Smart Entrepreneur* (Addicus Books Inc 1998).

Harvard Business Review on Entrepreneurship (Harvard Business School Press 1999).

Harvard Business Review on Leadership (Harvard Business School Press 1998).

Hesselbein, Frances, Goldsmith, Marshall and Beckard, Richard (editors), *The Drucker Foundations: The Organisation of the Future* (Jossey-Bass Publishers 1997).

Hisrich, Robert D. and Peters, Michael P., *Entrepreneurship* (Irwin/McCraw-Hill 1998).

Krass, Peter (editor), *The Book of Business Wisdom* (John Wiley & Son, Inc 1997).

Kotter, John P., *Matshushita Leadership* (Simon & Schuster 1997).

Levinson, Jay Conrad, *The Way of the Guerilla: Achieveing Success and Balance as an Entrepreneur in the 21st Century* (Houghton Mifflin Co 1997).

Lewis, Gareth, *The Mentoring Manager: Strategies for Fostering Talent and Spreading Knowledge* (Pitman Publishing 1996).

McGrath, Rita Gunther and Macmillan, Ian, *The Entrepreneurial Mindset* (Harvard Business School Press 2000).

Matshushita, Konosuke, *Velvet Glove, Iron Fist* (PHP Institute 1991).

Matshushita, Konosuke, *People before Products* (PHP Institute 1991).

Miner, John B., *The 4 Routes to Entrepreneurial Success* (Berrett Koehler Publishers 1996).

Morrell, Marget and Capparell, Stephanie, *Shackleton's Way* (Nicholas Brealey Publishing 2001).

Owen, Hilarie, *In Search of Leaders* (John Wiley and Sons Ltd 2000).

Packard, David, *The HP Way: How Bill Hewlett and I Built Our Company* (HarperCollins Publishers 1996).

Sewell, Carl and brown, Paul B., *Customers for Life* (Pocket Books 1998).

Viney, John, *Drive: Leadership in Business and Beyond* (Bloomsbury Publishing 1999).

Waitley, Denis, *Empires of the Mind: Lessons to Lead and Succeed in a Knowledge Based World* (Nicholas Brealey Publishing 1996).

COLIN TURNER

The Teachings of Billionaire Yen Tzu
Volumes I & II

"Hooks like a thriller you can't put down!
That a book can succeed in being authoritative about
success, business, lifestyle and spirituality is
impressive. That it's also engrossing, inspiring and
upbeat makes it essential for everyone" *Time Out*

**The Teachings of Yen Tzu shakes the very pillars of modern
thinking and practice. With esoteric secrets, enlightening stories
and insightful wisdom, its provocative lessons present a forgotten
yet powerful alchemy for meaning, purpose and prosperity.**

"As I am convinced the key to long-term success is a
secure philosophical and ethical background, I was delighted
to read this book" *Sir John Harvey-Jones*

A legend tells of a famous Academy founded some 2,500 years ago
by an immensely successful Patriarch, *Yen Tzu*, teaching the secrets
of a paradoxical philosophy that developed self-mastery through
individual inner understanding. Such a level of understanding was
instrumental in *Yen Tzu* becoming Ancient China's first commercial
billionaire; though such success inevitably attracted the attention of
an aspiring Emperor. History records that in the year 213BCE almost
all remnants of this ancient teaching were destroyed by the ruthless
Qin Shi Huang, famous for the army of life-size Terracotta Warriors.
In an attempt to save them from destruction, valuable scrolls were
hidden in hollowed walls, a time-honoured custom utilised over the
ages. History records that the Qin Dynasty lasted only during his
lifetime, a vivid reminder that motives seeking control are always
short-lived. Unwittingly, Qin destroyed the very wisdom that would
have been his greatest strength as a leader. Clearly, the application of
a new thinking and practice is as valid now as it was to prosperity
over two millennia ago.

www.21stcenturybooks.uk.com

TURNER
COLIN

Swimming with Piranha makes You Hungry

INTERNATIONAL BESTSELLER

Highly Recommended
Financial Times

Brilliant!
Daily Mail

Swimming with Piranha makes you Hungry is a
metaphorical must read –
a unique book humorously illustrated and packed
priceless advice – essential facts to enjoy life more,
less and *have more money!*

Discover powerful practical secrets to simplifying

Know the Seven Proven Laws vital for gaining we

This book is *guaranteed* to improve the quality of yo
and *increase* your disposable income!

www.21stcenturybooks.uk.com

T$\underset{\text{COLIN}}{U}$RNER

The Teachings of Billionaire Yen Tzu
Volumes I & II

"Hooks like a thriller you can't put down!
That a book can succeed in being authoritative about
success, business, lifestyle and spirituality is
impressive. That it's also engrossing, inspiring and
upbeat makes it essential for everyone" *Time Out*

**The Teachings of Yen Tzu shakes the very pillars of modern
thinking and practice. With esoteric secrets, enlightening stories
and insightful wisdom, its provocative lessons present a forgotten
yet powerful alchemy for meaning, purpose and prosperity.**

"As I am convinced the key to long-term success is a
secure philosophical and ethical background, I was delighted
to read this book" *Sir John Harvey-Jones*

A legend tells of a famous Academy founded some 2,500 years ago
by an immensely successful Patriarch, *Yen Tzu*, teaching the secrets
of a paradoxical philosophy that developed self-mastery through
individual inner understanding. Such a level of understanding was
instrumental in *Yen Tzu* becoming Ancient China's first commercial
billionaire; though such success inevitably attracted the attention of
an aspiring Emperor. History records that in the year 213BCE almost
all remnants of this ancient teaching were destroyed by the ruthless
Qin Shi Huang, famous for the army of life-size Terracotta Warriors.
In an attempt to save them from destruction, valuable scrolls were
hidden in hollowed walls, a time-honoured custom utilised over the
ages. History records that the Qin Dynasty lasted only during his
lifetime, a vivid reminder that motives seeking control are always
short-lived. Unwittingly, Qin destroyed the very wisdom that would
have been his greatest strength as a leader. Clearly, the application of
a new thinking and practice is as valid now as it was to prosperity
over two millennia ago.

www.21stcenturybooks.uk.com

COLIN TURNER

Swimming with Piranha makes You Hungry

INTERNATIONAL BESTSELLER

Highly Recommended
Financial Times

Brilliant!
Daily Mail

Swimming with Piranha makes you Hungry is a
metaphorical must read –
a unique book humorously illustrated and packed with
priceless advice – essential facts to enjoy life more, work
less and *have more money!*

Discover powerful practical secrets to simplifying life.

Know the Seven Proven Laws vital for gaining wealth.

This book is *guaranteed* to improve the quality of your life;
and *increase* your disposable income!

www.21stcenturybooks.uk.com

T<small>COLIN</small>URNER

Made for Life

INTERNATIONAL BESTSELLER

One of the classic tales of wisdom
***Made for life* is both profound and extraordinary.**

Delving deep, yet never becoming buried, this self-psychotherapy masterpiece provides simple answers to complex questions...those that *everyone* asks of themselves at quiet reflective times.

'A unique book and most of all it delivers
a very important message. You will love it'
URI GELLER

'I doubt very much whether anyone's life
will remain unchanged after reading it'
HERE'S HEALTH

'A profound, contemplative story'
WAYNE DYER

'If you are looking for answers in your life –
this little book speaks volumes'
STUART WILDE

www.21stcenturybooks.uk.com